**CANADIAN
RED CROSS**

Babysitter's Manual

Katherine Aspden

Name

StayWell

StayWell

Copyright © 2011 The Canadian Red Cross Society

The Canadian Red Cross Society has made reasonable efforts to ensure the contents of this publication are accurate and reflect the latest in available scientific research on the topic as of the date published. The information contained in this publication may change as new scientific research becomes available. Certain techniques described in this publication are designed for use in lifesaving situations. However, the Canadian Red Cross Society cannot guarantee that the use of such techniques will prevent personal injury or loss of life.

This publication is available in English and French

Design by Sarah Battersby
Illustrations by Christine Tripp
Printing/Binding by Kromar Printing

Printed in Canada by:
The StayWell Health Company Ltd.
2 Quebec Street, Suite 107, Guelph, ON N1H 2T3
A division of
StayWell
780 Township Line Road, Yardley, PA 19067-4200 USA

National Library of Canada Cataloguing in Publication
    Babysitter's manual / Canadian Red Cross.
ISBN 978-1-58480-161-0
    1. Babysitting. 2. First aid in illness and injury.
I. Canadian Red Cross Society
HQ769.5.B29 2003   649'.1'0248   C2003-905670-8

12 13 14 15 / 2 3 4 5

MIX
Paper from responsible sources
FSC
www.fsc.org   FSC® C103113

Acknowledgements

Over the past 65 years, the Canadian Red Cross First Aid Programs have developed and grown. Each time a program is revised, its foundation is built on the great work completed in the previous revision. We would like to acknowledge everyone who worked on the programs and products before us.

This project was completed because of the creative vision, ongoing support, and dedication of our publishing partner StayWell, the Canadian Red Cross National Medical Advisory Committee (NMAC), and the National First Aid Technical Advisory Group.

NMAC reviewed the content of the program and was made up of Brendan J. Hughes, MD, CCFP, and Andrew MacPherson, MD, CCFP-EM.

The National First Aid Technical Advisory Group was responsible for providing overall leadership, dedication, and direction. The group includes Bev Glass, Chair, Patrick Boucher, Blair Doyle, Dominique Graf, Kevin Holder, Jeff Horseman, Sioban Kennedy, Jason Oliver, Julie Poirier, Kathy Sampson, and Kevin Sanford.

The Canadian Medical Association, the Canadian Association of Fire Chiefs, the Industrial Accident Prevention Association, and SMARTRISK are pleased to support the important work of the Canadian Red Cross in developing this *Babysitter's Manual.*

External review and guidance were provided by the following individuals:

Yvonne Kelly
Masters of Education candidate

Anne McRuer
Girl Guides of Canada
Program Coordinator

Valerie Mason
Girl Guides of Canada
Training Resource Co-rdinator

Ian Mitchell
Scouts Canada
National Program Director

Shirley Gallant
Fire Prevention Canada
Manager

Paula Hadden-Jokiel
Health Canada
Senior Policy Analyst
Middle Childhood and Adolescence Section (MCAS)
Strategic Policy and Research Section (SPRS)
Division of Childhood and Adolescence (DCA)

Dr. Robert Conn
SMARTRISK Foundation
President/CEO

Kathy Blair
SMARTRISK Foundation
Writer

Amy Zierler
Laveena Sethia
Nicole Beben
Rebecca Nesdale-Tucker
(Injury Prevention Information Team)
Safe Kids Canada

Dr. Judy Guernsey
Canadian Agricultural Safety Association
Chair

About the Canadian Red Cross

Our Mission*

In keeping with the International Federation of Red Cross and Red Crescent Societies, the Canadian Red Cross's mission is:

to improve the lives of the vulnerable by mobilizing
the power of humanity

* provisionally approved by the Board of Governors, December 2002

How We Help

The Canadian Red Cross is dedicated to helping make families, schools, and communities safer at home and around the world.

Disaster Management

Canadian Red Cross helps people affected by emergencies and disasters. Red Cross works with governments and other humanitarian organizations to ensure people's basic needs are met – food, clothing, shelter, first aid, emotional support, and family reunification.

International Operations

The Canadian Red Cross works overseas in situations of war and natural disaster to bring urgently needed relief items, reunite families, and help rebuild communities. Each year, Canadian Red Cross sends about 100 professional relief workers on overseas missions.

First Aid Programs

The aim of the Canadian Red Cross First Aid Programs is to reduce death and suffering due to injury and sudden illness by training as many Canadians as possible in first aid.

Swimming and Water Safety Program

Thanks to the work of the Canadian Red Cross Water Safety Program, more than 32 million Canadians have, since 1946, learned how to swim and safely enjoy water activities.

RespectED: Violence and Abuse Prevention

This award winning Red Cross service has helped more than one million Canadian youth and adults understand abuse, harassment, and interpersonal violence issues.

Homecare Services

The Canadian Red Cross's homecare services enhance people's well-being and dignity, be they frail or elderly, people with disabilities or at home with an illness.

Red Cross Fundamental Principles

All Red Cross programs and activities are guided by the Fundamental Principles, which allow us to provide help to whomever needs it, whatever their race, political beliefs, religion, social status, or culture.

A formal definition hangs in most Red Cross offices, but a simpler interpretation comes from the Tanzanian Red Cross:

HUMANITY We serve people, but not systems.

IMPARTIALITY We care for the victims and the aggressors alike.

NEUTRALITY We take initiatives, but never take sides.

INDEPENDENCE We bow to needs, but not kings.

VOLUNTARY SERVICE We work around the clock, but never for personal gain.

UNITY We have many talents, but a single idea.

UNIVERSALITY We respect nations, but our work knows no bounds.

Contents

Chapter 5

Caring for School-Aged Children

Chapter 6

Injury Is No Accident: Creating Safe Environments

Chapter 7

How to Handle Emergencies and First Aid

Chapter 8

Special Considerations

CHAPTER 1

Getting Started

The Business of Babysitting

So you've decided to become a babysitter—congratulations! Babysitting is fun and rewarding, but it's also an important job.

Parents and guardians of the children you babysit depend on you to supervise their children and keep them safe while they are away. You are a leader because children look to you as the responsible person in charge. A good leader is confident and is comfortable being in charge because he or she uses good decision-making skills and always thinks about safety. This Babysitting Course will help you know how to make good decisions and will help you have confidence in your skills and ability to be a successful babysitter!

How to Use the Canadian Red Cross Babysitter's Manual

You will use this *Babysitter's Manual* when you take the Canadian Red Cross Babysitting Course. There are several activities in the manual that you will do in class. Go ahead and write on these pages for class activities. This book belongs to YOU and will be useful to keep in your babysitting kit to take on your babysitting jobs.

In this course, you will learn about starting out as a babysitter and how to care for BABIES, TODDLERS, PRESCHOOLERS, and SCHOOL-AGED CHILDREN. You will also learn about making a safe ENVIRONMENT when you babysit and how to handle emergencies and give first aid.

You will see words throughout this manual in CAPS. These are words that you might need help with and are explained in the Glossary at the back of this manual.

What Makes a Babysitter Great?

A great babysitter is someone who is responsible, dependable, and trustworthy. A great babysitter sets a good example and is a ROLE MODEL for children. While on the job, a great babysitter always acts in a PROFESSIONAL way and is a leader.

Leadership

The symbol to the left represents LEADERSHIP. A babysitter shows leadership when he or she ensures children's safety, provides care and FIRST AID, makes good decisions, and demonstrates professionalism. You will see this symbol throughout this manual next to leadership tips.

You can be a great babysitter by:

- Keeping yourself and the children safe;
- Communicating well with both the children and the parents or guardians;
- Being interested in the children you are babysitting;

- Making decisions carefully;
- Guiding the children's behaviour appropriately;
- Respecting the DIVERSITY of people and households;
- Using tools that can help you do a better job, such as this manual; and
- Evaluating yourself after each job and making improvement as needed.

Benefits of Being a Babysitter

There are many benefits of being a babysitter. It's a great way for you to be with kids, learn some new caring skills, have fun, and gain job experience. It's also a way for you to earn a little money.

Business Basics

Before you begin your career as a professional babysitter, think about the type of babysitting job you would like to have and think you can handle. Also think about the type of job you think might be too much for you to handle. If you have no babysitting experience, start out by babysitting just one child for 2 or 3 hours, perhaps while the parent or guardian is present or nearby. As you feel comfortable, you may take a job that is a little longer and perhaps has more than one child. Only agree to a babysitting job that you are comfortable taking!

Before agreeing to a job, talk about your fee with the hiring parents. The number of children, how many hours, the location of the job, and the tasks you may be asked to perform, such as giving baths or cooking dinner, may be factors when determining how much money to charge for a babysitting job. Most babysitters are paid on an

hourly basis. The current rate for babysitting in your area is between $_____ and $_____ per hour. Make sure that you and the hiring parents agree to the rate before you accept the job.

Create a Résumé

Use the blank RÉSUMÉ on p. 5 to help you apply for babysitting jobs. Fill in the blanks to create your résumé. Then you can print or type your résumé on a clean sheet of paper to give to parents who may want to hire you.

Notes:

_____

_____

_____

_____

_____

_____

_____

_____

_____

_____

_____

_____

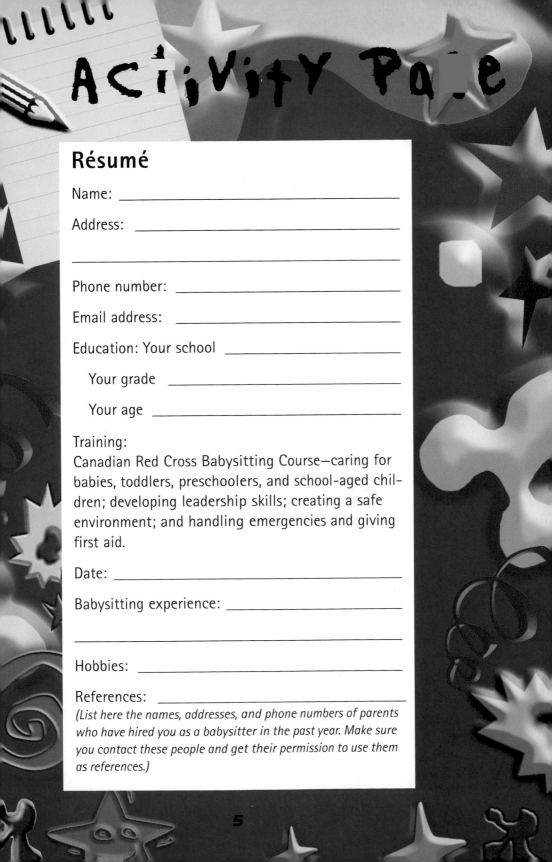

Activity Page

Résumé

Name: _____

Address: _____

_____

Phone number: _____

Email address: _____

Education: Your school _____

   Your grade _____

   Your age _____

Training:
Canadian Red Cross Babysitting Course—caring for babies, toddlers, preschoolers, and school-aged children; developing leadership skills; creating a safe environment; and handling emergencies and giving first aid.

Date: _____

Babysitting experience: _____

_____

Hobbies: _____

References: _____
(List here the names, addresses, and phone numbers of parents who have hired you as a babysitter in the past year. Make sure you contact these people and get their permission to use them as references.)

Professional Behaviour

What does it mean to act in a professional way? Babysitting is a job that requires a lot of responsibility. People who hire you trust you to keep their children safe and give good care. They are looking for a person who behaves in a professional manner when they hire a babysitter. Part of behaving professionally is being trustworthy. A babysitter who is trustworthy tells the truth, takes responsibility seriously, and follows the parents' instructions.

Parents want a babysitter who is mature and is capable of **SUPERVISING** their children and making sure they are safe. They also want a babysitter who is dependable. A dependable babysitter is someone who is always on time and keeps appointments. Parents also want a babysitter who is good at the job and is kind and respectful to their children. This is what being a professional babysitter is all about!

Professional Behaviour Pointers

- Respect the household routines and rules.
- Give your full attention to the children. Never invite friends over unless you have permission from the parents. Stay awake unless you have permission to sleep. Children come before TV or homework.
- Only babysit when you are well. Tell parents right away that you cannot babysit instead of waiting to see if you feel better.
- If you must cancel, give as much advance notice as possible. It's hard to find another babysitter on short notice.
- Never look through belongings or rooms where you babysit.
- Always arrive at the job early or on time.

- Clean up any mess you make or any mess the children make while in your care.
- Ask what you are allowed to eat.
- Ask whether you may use the TV, DVD player, video game console, or computer.
- Always treat the family with respect.
- Dress for the job and the weather.

Self-Evaluation After the Job

After finishing a babysitting job, ask yourself these questions:

❏ How do I feel about this job? Did I do well?

❏ Did I do everything the parents asked me to do?

❏ How did the children respond to me?

❏ Were there any problems?

❏ Did anything happen that I did not know how to handle?

❏ What are some good things that happened?

❏ What did I like and dislike about this job?

❏ What would I do differently for the next babysitting job?

❏ What could I have done to make this job go better?

❏ If this family offers me another job, will I take it? Why or why not?

❏ Other comments:

∿∿∿⟩ *Your Role*

Wanted: Professional babysitter for active children. Babysitter must be dependable and trustworthy and must like kids. Leadership skills preferred. Those interested in ignoring the rules of the house need not apply.

If you think this job description suits you, you probably have what it takes to be a good babysitter. If you choose to make babysitting your profession for the next few years, this manual will help you start your babysitting business, teach you communication and leadership skills, and teach you about safety, child care, and getting along with children.

Finding Work

The best way to find babysitting jobs is through word-of-mouth. Talk with your parents about which families you know who may need babysitters. Tell neighbours whom you know that you are looking for work as a babysitter. Ask your friends who babysit to give your name if they can't accept a job.

For your own safety, don't advertise in a newspaper, on a bulletin board or over the internet. Never give out your name, phone number, or address to anyone you don't know.

The first time someone asks you to babysit, ask lots of questions.

Get to know the routines and rules, safety, and childcare information. When you talk to parents for the first time, ask where they got your name. Suggest meeting ahead of the babysitting date. Ensure your parents are okay with you going to

meet them, especially if neither you or your parents know the person calling. The children's parents can give you all the information you need to know. This is also a chance to meet the children and make friends. If you can't meet ahead of the date, arrange to arrive at least a half-hour before the parents leave so you have a chance to get information you need.

Parents will appreciate that you are responsible and well prepared.

Phone Interview

Questions to ask:

1. What are your names (parents), phone number, and address?

2. What is the date and time of the job?

3. When will I start and finish work?

4. How many children will I look after? What are their names? How old are they?

5. Do any of the children have special needs?

6. How will I get to your home and back safely?

7. I usually charge $_____, is that okay with you?

8. Are you expecting any household chores (such as walking the dog, doing dishes) to be done as part of the job?

9. May I come over a half-hour early to meet the children and discuss my checklist (see p. 10)?

10. May I have a friend over? (if necessary)

11. Are there any family pets? Are they friendly?

Rules and Routines

Parents must be clear about what they expect from you. They look after their children all the time, so they might forget to tell you everything you need to know. If they don't tell you what you need to know, you should ask questions.

Rules of the House

❐ What is the phone number where I can reach you?

❐ Whom should I call in case you are unavailable?

❐ What are the phone numbers for ambulance, police, poison control centre, fire department, children's doctor, neighbours?

❐ Where are the telephones?

❐ What parts of the house are off-limits?

❐ May I leave the house with the children? If yes, what places are okay with you?

❐ What foods are the children allowed to eat? What foods am I allowed to eat?

❐ Do any of the children have allergies?

❐ May I use the phone?

❐ Is there an extra key?

❐ Does a neighbour have an extra key?

❐ May I watch TV and use the computer?

❐ Are there any rules for the children using the telephone, stereo, video game console, TV, or computer?

❐ What behaviour management techniques do you use with your children (counting to 3, time outs)?

Safety Checklist

❒ Where are the first aid kit or first aid materials kept? (For common items in a first aid kit, see p. 104 of this manual.)

❒ Can you show me the layout of the house?

❒ Where are the smoke alarms and fire extinguisher?

❒ Where do you keep a flashlight?

❒ What is the family's emergency fire escape route?

Routines

❒ What are the children's bedtime routines?

❒ Are there any special toys that the children like to play with?

❒ Are there any medical conditions or medications (e.g., inhaler or EpiPen®) that I should be aware of? If the child is taking medication, where is it kept? Ask for very clear instructions.

Safety Tips

Safety is important for both you and the children you babysit.

- Know the parents who hire you to babysit their children.
- Tell your parents the address and phone number of the house where you will be babysitting, the times you will be there, and when you will be home. Also make sure you know where your parents will be while you are babysitting in case you need to contact them.
- Before you accept a job, make sure you have a way of getting to and from the job safely.
- Dress appropriately. Don't wear anything that would scratch or hurt you or the children.
- Only babysit when you are well.
- Do not drink alcohol, smoke, or use drugs.
- Take your *Babysitter's Manual* with you to each babysitting job.
- Know how much responsibility you can handle and only accept babysitting jobs that you are sure about.

Be Confident and Comfortable!

This course will help you develop the leadership skills you will need to become a great babysitter. This training will help prepare you to handle each babysitting situation and will enable you to have confidence in your abilities.

If you feel uncomfortable babysitting for a family, politely tell them that you won't be able to babysit for them anymore. Talk to your parents or a trusted adult about your feelings.

Family's Expectations

The people who hire you trust you with their children. Finding babysitters who are professional about their work is hard. Once they find a babysitter they trust and their children like, they'll stick with that babysitter.

Parents have a right to expect a babysitter who has the right qualities for the job.

Are you someone who is:

Interested in children?	yes ❐	no ❐
Able to supervise children safely?	yes ❐	no ❐
Honest and reliable?	yes ❐	no ❐
In good mental and physical health?	yes ❐	no ❐
Able to carry out instructions?	yes ❐	no ❐
Able to think clearly in emergencies?	yes ❐	no ❐
Able to recognize safety hazards?	yes ❐	no ❐
Able to provide simple first aid?	yes ❐	no ❐
Able to prepare basic meals?	yes ❐	no ❐

Able to play with children?	yes ❑	no ❑
Able to communicate well?	yes ❑	no ❑
Able to discuss job responsibilities and policies?	yes ❑	no ❑

Parents also have a right to privacy. Remember to respect someone else's belongings by not looking through their things. Also, avoid gossiping about the family with your friends.

Respecting Diversity

Some people have a lot in common, but not everyone is the same. People look different, act differently, and believe different things. This is called diversity. Diversity is good because if the world were full of the same kind of people, it would be a very boring place to live in. You may see diversity in the children you babysit.

Cultural diversity. A family that you babysit for may be from another country or a different culture than your own. The family might wear different clothes or speak another language or with an accent. They might eat different foods and do things in a way that you are not used to. Learning new words and other customs is fun! Be respectful of the family's differences, and don't be afraid to ask questions.

Religious beliefs. Your religious beliefs may be different from those of a family that you babysit for. The children you babysit may celebrate different holidays and have different traditions. Be respectful of all families and their religious beliefs.

Family members. Each family is different in some way. Some of the children you babysit may live with both parents or only one parent. Other children may live with grandparents or with other family members who are not the parents. Be respectful of family members.

Family lifestyle. You may notice that some families that you babysit for have different types of houses and cars and the children have different types of clothing or toys. It's your job to do your best on each babysitting job and give the same care to all children, no matter how many or what kind of things they have.

Children's Expectations

Children don't know what makes a "good" and a "bad" babysitter, but they do know the difference between a "fun" and a "boring" babysitter.

Children also want to feel happy and secure. They want a babysitter who:

- Knows the household routines and rules;
- Makes them feel comfortable and secure;
- Shows an interest in them;
- Plays with them; and
- Knows what to do in an EMERGENCY.

A happy child is the best advertisement for a babysitter. Keeping children safe and happy will make your business grow.

Children Are Diverse

Age. Children are different at different ages. For example, an eight-year-old boy does not play the same way he did when he was four. It's normal to have interests that change. It's a part of growing up.

Developmental stages. Most babies and children grow in similar ways. They can do the same kinds of things at certain ages. This is called DEVELOPMENTAL STAGES. For example, at about 9 to 12 months of age, most babies can pull themselves up into a standing position. It's important to remember that even though some of the children you babysit may be the same age or developmental stage, each may act in different ways.

Boys and girls. You may notice that the boys and girls you babysit may like the same things and act in similar ways. Don't assume that a girl or boy won't like to play a particular game or activity.

Individual differences. Not everyone likes the same things. That's what makes people individuals. Also, some children may be frightened easily, while others aren't. It's important that you realize that even children from the same family are individuals and may think differently and react differently to situations.

Your Family's Expectations

You will probably need to work out with your parents how your babysitting business fits in with your schoolwork and your family responsibilities.

Your parents have a right to know:

- Where you are;
- Who you are babysitting for;
- What time you'll be home; and
- How you will be getting home safely.

Notes:

_____

_____

_____

_____

_____

_____

_____

_____

_____

_____

_____

_____

_____

_____

_____

_____

_____

_____

_____

_____

_____

CHAPTER 2

Caring for Babies

Babies may be too young to talk, but they can communicate in their own way. When you babysit a baby, talk to him or her. Babies also need to be with others. For example, when they wake up from a nap, they like to be held. This lets them know that they are not alone and makes them feel secure. By interacting with and giving attention to the baby you babysit, you can make sure he or she is safe.

Most babies love to touch and hold things, and they often put things in their mouth. But every child is different. Your job as a babysitter is to get to know the children you look after and appreciate their differences. Here are some characteristics of babies.

Stages for Babies

A baby (newborn to 12 months) may do many or all of the following:

- Reaches for objects
- Holds small toys
- Lifts chest off ground
- Can roll over
- Puts hands and objects in mouth
- Rolls or wiggles toward toys
- Holds head steady (at about six months old)

- Grabs at spoons
- Can sit up
- Can crawl
- Can crawl up stairs, but not down
- Can be shy around strangers
- Pulls up to a standing position (at about 9 to 12 months old)
- Side steps while holding onto furniture
- Starts to walk
- Says a few words
- Reacts to "no"

Holding
Cradle Hold

Most babies like being held, although some may not. Respect individual differences.

1. Talk in a soft voice while you slide one hand under the baby's bottom. Spread out the fingers of your other hand and slide it under the neck and upper shoulders.

2. Lift the baby slowly and gently and hold him or her near your body. Your arms should form a cosy hammock for the baby with the head resting near the inside of your elbow.

Shoulder Hold

From the cradle hold,

3. While still supporting the baby's head and neck, shift
him or her gently so that the chest and head rest
against your shoulder.

Remember! A small baby cannot support its head or
neck until he or she is four to six months old. Always
support the head and neck when holding small babies!

Diapers

It's a good idea to ask parents to show you how to change their baby's diaper. Everyone has a slightly different way of doing the same job!

1. Gather everything you need before you start to change the diaper, such as two diapers, baby wipes or cloths, cream (depending on what the parents told you), and a towel for drying. Before picking up the baby from the crib after a nap, set up the diaper changing area.

- Never leave a baby alone on a changing area or bed! They can squirm and roll off if you're not careful. If the phone rings, let it ring!
- Be sure to use the safety straps or guardrails on a changing area to secure the baby.
- Always leave one hand on the baby at all times to keep him or her safe.

2. There are two common types of diapers: cloth diapers with Velcro fasteners and disposable diapers.

3. Take off the wet or dirty diaper. Set the dirty diaper out of the way where the baby can't reach it.

4. With one hand, lift the baby's ankles to lift the legs and hips. Clean the bottom with a baby wipe or warm cloth. Wipe the baby from front to back to prevent infections. Dry the baby too. When changing a boy, keep him covered with a baby wipe or diaper as much as possible during the change to avoid being sprayed.

5. If the parents tell you to put cream or powder on the baby, do it now.

6. Raise the baby's heels to slide a clean diaper under the bottom. The sticky tabs should be on either side of the baby's hips. Open the tape or Velcro and stick it to the front. Repeat for the other side.

7. Get rid of the dirty diaper once the baby is dressed and off the changing area. Follow the instructions the parents gave you for taking care of dirty diapers.

8. Wash your hands and the baby's hands.

- Since babies like to put their hands in their mouths, it's a good idea to wash babies' hands often, especially after changing a diaper. This will help keep the baby from getting sick. Use a washcloth, soap, and lukewarm or cool water to wash the baby's hands.

9. Put all of the baby products that you have used out of baby's reach. Products like baby oil are very dangerous if swallowed by a baby.

Dressing

Babies can be messy, especially after eating, and often need their clothes changed several times a day. If you need to change a baby's clothes and the parents haven't left clothing out, find something that is easy to put on and comfortable for the baby to wear, such as sleepers with a zipper or snaps.

1. Get all the clothes that you need together before you start. It depends on the weather, of course, but the baby will likely need an undershirt, a shirt, overalls or pants, socks, and maybe a sweater. Babies don't need and don't like mountains of clothes! Dress the baby as warmly as you are dressed. For babies younger than six months, add one more layer.

2. If it's up to you to choose the clothing, avoid anything that must be pulled tightly over the head like turtlenecks or sweaters. Outfits that snap up the legs or the shoulder are easier for changing diapers later.

3. Some babies hate being naked because it can make them feel cold and unprotected, so move quickly and with confidence.

4. A baby's arms and legs are very flexible. Be gentle as you slip the baby into his or her clothes.

5. Put the dirty clothes in a laundry hamper or laundry room, and be sure to tell the parents when they come home.

Feeding

If you are expected to feed a small baby, make sure you have clear instructions before the parents leave. Babies have very specific diets; make sure that the foods you give are safe for them. Only give the foods the parents tell you to give.

Bottle Feeding

1. Wash your hands before handling any part of a baby's bottle.

2. Mix the **FORMULA** according to the parent's instructions. Babies can drink breast milk, or liquid or powdered formula.

3. To warm the milk, put the bottle of milk or formula in a small saucepan, bowl, or a bottle warmer if the parents use one. Pour in hot tap water to surround the bottle and warm the milk.

Note: Milk that is heated in a microwave can feel fine on the outside but can be very hot on the inside. This uneven heating is why using a microwave for heating milk is not recommended.

4. Gently shake the bottle to make sure it is evenly heated.

5. Test the temperature of the milk by sprinkling a few drops on the inside of your wrists where your skin is most sensitive. The milk should be lukewarm.

6. Sit down with the baby in your arms. Tilt the bottle so the nipple is full of milk. Put it in his or her mouth. If the baby cries and won't take the bottle, you may need to calm him or her down by rocking a little bit. For very young babies, touch their cheek with the nipple. They will turn their head toward the nipple to suck.

7. If the baby spits out the nipple it could mean several things—that the nipple is clogged, that he or she has to burp, or it may mean that the baby isn't hungry anymore. Never force a baby to finish a bottle.

8. Ask parents if the baby needs to burp. When the baby has finished a third of the bottle, place him or her upright with the head on your shoulder. Warning! Place a cloth between you and the baby. The baby

may spit up and things could get messy! Pat or rub the baby's back gently until you hear a burp. Repeat this when the bottle is two-thirds done and when he or she is finished.

9. Never leave a baby alone with a bottle! The baby could throw up and choke on the VOMIT!

Spoon Feeding

1. If parents have asked you to spoon feed the baby, start by placing the baby food in a small container.

2. Put the container into a larger container of hot water to heat it up.

3. Some families warm up baby food in their microwave oven. You must be very careful if you use the microwave to heat baby food because it can heat up foods unevenly. You might test a tiny bit of cereal and find that it is lukewarm. An inch away, the cereal may be very hot. Make sure you mix the food thoroughly and test the temperature of the food on the inside of your wrist before giving it to the baby.

4. Gather everything you will need on a table beside the high chair. Put the baby in the high chair and secure the straps. Place a bib around the baby's neck. You should have a cloth handy for spills—there will be many.

5. Some babies may have a special feeding spoon they use. Don't expect the baby to eat all of the food. When a baby cries or turns away from the food, that means he or she doesn't want to eat. Don't force the baby to eat more than he or she wants.

6. It's important not to leave the baby alone in the high chair. Keep hot foods out of reach.

7. Put the dishes and utensils in the sink and out of the baby's reach.

Activity Page

Food Find

Circle the appropriate foods for a baby from the selections below.

Sleeping

Before the parents leave, ask them to walk you through the bedtime routine. What time does the baby go to sleep? Should I leave the lights on or off? What's the baby's favourite toy or blanket? If the baby cries should I go right away or wait? How long should I wait? Does the baby take a soother to bed?

Remove toys and stuffed animals from the crib.

Before bedtime do quiet activities such as reading or singing to help relax the baby. Noisy play may overexcite a baby rather than tire him or her out.

1. When babies are sleepy they may rub their eyes or suck their thumbs. They may also be fussy or cranky.

2. Use a gentle voice and move slowly while going through the bedtime routine. By being calm you will help calm the baby.

3. Make sure the crib has nothing dangerous in it (small objects).

4. Put the baby down in the crib. Always place babies on their backs. Make sure the sides of the crib are locked in place. Say goodnight. Leave the room.

5. If you are watching TV or listening to music, make sure the volume is low so you can hear if the baby cries.

6. Some babies cry for a few minutes at bedtime or may wake up and cry. If he or she cries, check on the baby. Enter the baby's room quietly, keep the lights off, and talk quietly to calm the baby.

7. Quietly check on the baby every half-hour while he or she is asleep.

Have one of the parents show you how to work the crib ahead of time. Also, the parents may use a baby monitor. A baby monitor enables the parents or you, the babysitter, to keep tabs on a sleeping baby while you are in another room. If the parents would like you to use their baby monitor, be sure to ask them to show you how it works.

Crying

Crying is the only way small babies can tell the world around them that something is wrong or that they need something. Ask the parents what they normally do when the baby cries.

1. Things to check:
- Did the baby's favourite blanket or soother fall out of the crib?
- Is the diaper clean and dry?
- Is the baby hungry?
- Does the baby need to burp?

2. If you don't know why the baby is crying, don't take it personally. The baby is not crying because he or she doesn't like you or because you're doing something wrong. Try rocking or walking the baby. Talk in a soothing voice. Sometimes babies are fussy for no apparent reason.

Soothers should not have strings attached. Before giving a soother to a baby, check to make sure that it has no cracks or tears.

When you've tried everything—feeding, changing the diaper, walking, rocking, and cuddling—and the baby still won't stop crying, stay calm. If you are upset and angry, the baby will sense your feelings and will likely cry more. Place the baby on his or her back in a safe place and let him or her "cry it out" for a few minutes, while you stay nearby. Relax and take some deep breaths and then try again to soothe the baby.

Never shake a baby or a child, no matter what. Shaking is very dangerous and can cause serious injury or death. Remember, no matter how you are feeling—never shake a baby or a child. Take a break, never shake!

3. If the baby keeps crying and the cries are piercing or uncontrollable, call his or her parents. Don't be embarrassed. They will either tell you over the phone what to do, or they will come home.

Don't ever shake a child or baby. Take a break, never shake!

Getting Along

Small babies like anything that appeals to their senses of sound, sight, and touch. It's a good idea to bring a babysitting kit with you to each job. Fill the kit with toys and activities that are appropriate for the ages and developmental stages of the children you are babysitting. When babysitting a baby, pack a board book and toys that make sounds or music. You may also want to gather scrap materials of different textures for touching: velvet, terry cloth, fur, satin, and wool for the baby to play with. Remember, it's also a good idea to disinfect the toys after each babysitting job.

Having Fun Together

Babies love faces and voices. They can play in their cribs or playpen by themselves with some toys, but they also like being where the action is.

Place the baby on a blanket on the floor where he or she can wiggle or move safely. The baby might like brightly coloured soft toys, musical toys, rattles, board books, blocks, pots and pans, balls, squeaky toys, and toys that pull apart and snap together. Most babies like games such as pat-a-cake, this little piggy, and peek-a-boo.

Creating a babysitting kit ahead of time is a great way to ensure you bring all the items you need to the job. Just fill a knapsack or backpack with your checklists, *Babysitter's Manual*, toys, first aid kit, and anything else you may need, and you're all set!

Activity Page

Be a Problem Solver

It's naptime for six-month-old Lily, so you gently place her on her back in the crib. As soon as you put her down, she begins to cry. As you pick her up again to try to soothe her, she stops crying. After a few moments of quiet, you lay her down in the crib again. She lets out a wail. What should you do?

Eight-month-old Nate has a dirty diaper. You carry him into the nursery and gently place him on the changing area. After securing the straps around him, you begin removing the dirty diaper. Just then, you realize that you have forgotten to get a clean diaper from the drawer across the room. What should you do?

_____

_____

_____

_____

_____

_____

_____

_____

_____

_____

Precautions for Babies

Babies love to touch and hold things. They especially like to put things in their mouth. Once they reach about three months of age, they can roll over. Constant supervision is the best precaution against injury.

Babies are at greatest danger from:

- Falling—Never leave a baby alone on a changing area, couch, or high chair. If you have to leave, take the baby with you or put him or her back in the crib or play pen. Always use the safety strap to keep the child sitting safely in high chairs and strollers.
- Crib injuries—Check the crib before putting the baby in. Make sure there are no small objects in the crib. Never put a pillow or heavy blankets in the crib. A baby can get tangled up or smothered. Use a light blanket only. Make sure window blind cords are not near the crib, as this is a strangulation hazard.
- Burns—Always watch a baby near the stove, fireplace, radiator, or baseboard heaters. Don't drink anything hot when you're near a baby. He or she may grab your cup or bump you and then get burned (or burn you). Be careful when washing a baby's hands; use a washcloth instead of holding the baby's hands under the faucet. Always use lukewarm or cool water.
- Inhaling, swallowing, or CHOKING on small objects and pieces of food—Never leave a baby alone with a bottle. Only give other foods if the parents have told you to. Look out for small objects on the floor that a baby could swallow.
- Getting fingers caught in doors or falling down stairs—Babies who crawl are fearless explorers. You won't be able to turn your back on them for an instant! Never leave a baby near open stairways. Be aware of electrical

outlets that are not covered. Never let a baby play near electrical outlets or cords. Keep babies away from cupboards that may contain dangerous substances. They are curious and may try to open cupboard doors, drawers, or doors that can close on little hands.

- **DROWNING**—You should never agree to give a baby a bath while you are babysitting. Babies can be scalded by water and can very easily drown. This is a responsibility for a parent or relative only.

Toys and Games for Babies

The best way to keep babies safe is to keep them happy and busy, and know what they are doing. That means choosing toys, games, and activities that are appropriate for their ages and abilities.

Toys and games for babies up to one year:

- Brightly coloured soft toys
- Musical toys
- Rattles
- Cloth books
- Crib toys
- Filling and dumping toys
- Toys (not too small) that pull apart and snap together
- Big blocks
- Board books
- "Pat-a-cake"
- "This little piggy"
- "Peek-a-boo"

Notes:

_____

_____

_____

_____

_____

_____

_____

_____

_____

_____

_____

_____

_____

_____

_____

_____

_____

_____

_____

_____

Activity Page

Matching Toy with Age

Draw lines to connect the baby with an appropriate toy. Put an "X" over the toy that is unsafe for any age.

Caring for Toddlers

Stages for Toddlers

A Toddler (one to three years) may do many or all of the following:

- Walks
- Feeds him- or herself
- Uses one- to three-word sentences
- Is determined to do things on their own
- Climbs on furniture
- Runs, skips, jumps, climbs, and gallops! (older toddler)
- Dresses self (with help)
- Brushes teeth (with help)

Most toddlers like to walk, climb, and explore. They may understand what you say, but they may only say a few words that only their parents understand. This can be frustrating for both the toddler and for you.

Diapers

Most toddlers still wear diapers. Unless they have a dirty diaper, you can change the diaper quickly and easily. Be sure to tell toddlers what you are going to do to get their cooperation. They probably even know how to get a clean diaper for you!

1. Get a clean diaper.

2. Unsnap or pull down his or her pants and remove the dirty diaper.

3. Get the toddler to lie down on his or her back. Lift the legs to clean him or her. Dry him or her off too.

4. Put the dry diaper around the toddler. Make sure the tape or Velcro attachments are at the back at hip level. Open the tape or Velcro and stick it to the front. Repeat for the other side.

5. Follow the instructions the parents gave you for taking care of dirty diapers.

6. Wash your hands and the toddler's hands.

7. After you have finished, put all of the baby products that you have used out of the toddler's reach. Products like baby oil are very dangerous if swallowed by a toddler.

Dressing

Parents may want you to help dress their toddler.

To undress a toddler:

1. Undo the snaps or buttons on the front of the shirt.

2. If the toddler is wearing a T-shirt or pullover shirt, gently slide one arm out of the sleeve and then slide out the other. Then, ease the shirt over the toddler's head, gently past one ear, and then the other.

To dress a toddler:

1. To put on a shirt that buttons, undo the buttons or snaps. Gather or scrunch up the length of one sleeve and reach through the sleeve to gently grab the toddler's hand. Gently pull the toddler's hand and arm through the sleeve. Pull the shirt around the back and do the same with the toddler's other arm. Snap or button the shirt.

2. To put on a T-shirt, stretch the neck of the shirt bigger so the toddler's head can easily fit through the opening. Gently pull the opening over the toddler's head being careful not to pull down on the ears and nose.

- After the toddler's head is through the opening, gently guide each arm through the sleeves.

3. Put the dirty laundry where the parents or guardians told you to put it.

Feeding

Toddlers may be able to eat by themselves in a high chair. They don't eat baby food any more, but they will need their food cut into tiny pieces or mashed a little bit. They especially like finger food that they can hold. Hard or solid foods like raw fruit or vegetables should be cut up in very small pieces. Hot dogs or sausages should be cut into long strips and then cut up into small pieces. Toddlers still need to wear a bib! And you should be prepared to clean the high chair, and around the high chair, thoroughly after mealtime.

Remember, toddlers should not be left alone in the high chair.

- Move the high chair away from the stove, electrical appliances, and hot liquids.
- Keep the high chair away from tables and walls so that the child cannot push the chair over.
- Do not allow the child to stand in the high chair. Secure the child in the high chair with safety straps. Make sure the toddler sits quietly when he or she eats. A toddler can easily choke if he or she walks or runs while eating.

Food Find

Circle the appropriate foods for a toddler from the selections below.

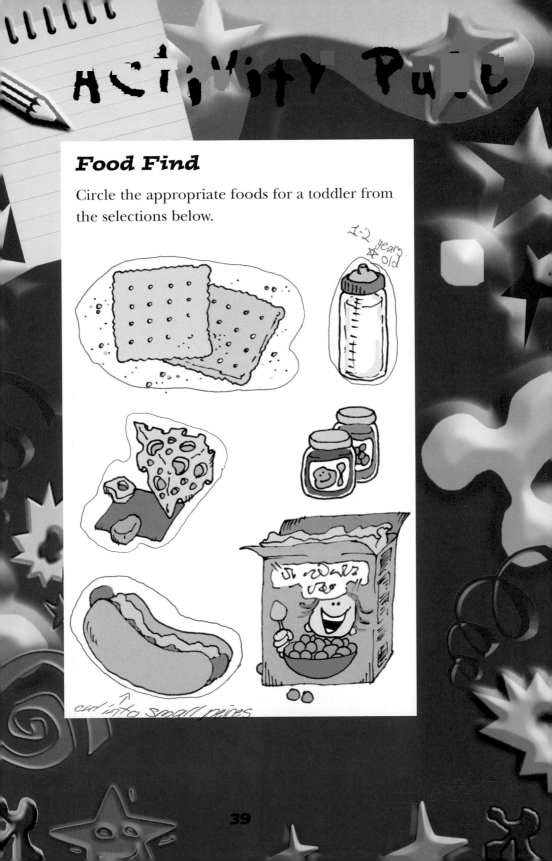

Choose quiet activities such as reading stories before bedtime.

Sleeping

Toddlers use up a lot of energy! They need their rest, but they don't always want to sleep. Ask the toddler's parents what his or her sleep time routine is and stick to it.

You can tell that toddlers are getting tired when they begin to rub their eyes, pull on their ears, or even have little circles around their eyes.

Help the toddler prepare for naptime and bedtime by choosing quiet activities such as reading stories or watching TV. You may think active play before sleep will tire him or her out. What really happens is that the toddler gets overexcited and can't sleep.

Be firm that it's time for sleep. Follow the toddler's normal routine, tell him or her that you're close by, and say goodnight.

Getting Along

What toddler doesn't love surprises? One way to be a success as a babysitter is to pack a babysitting kit with toys, books, stickers, stamps, and ideas for activities and games. Be clear with the children that these are your things for sharing and that you are taking them home with you. Also be sure that they are safe and appropriate for the toddler you are looking after.

Use your imagination. Be a pretend animal and make the toddler guess which one. Bring some children's books or playdough.

Having Fun Together

Most toddlers are very curious and get into trouble because they don't understand about safety. The

best way to keep them out of trouble is to play with them!

Toddlers you babysit may like action toys like trains, cars, telephones, toys to push and pull, dolls, building blocks, crafts, sand and water play, plastic dishes, musical instruments, and books. Toddlers love to put things in their mouth. Keep toys with small parts or batteries out of their reach.

Notes:

_____

_____

_____

_____

_____

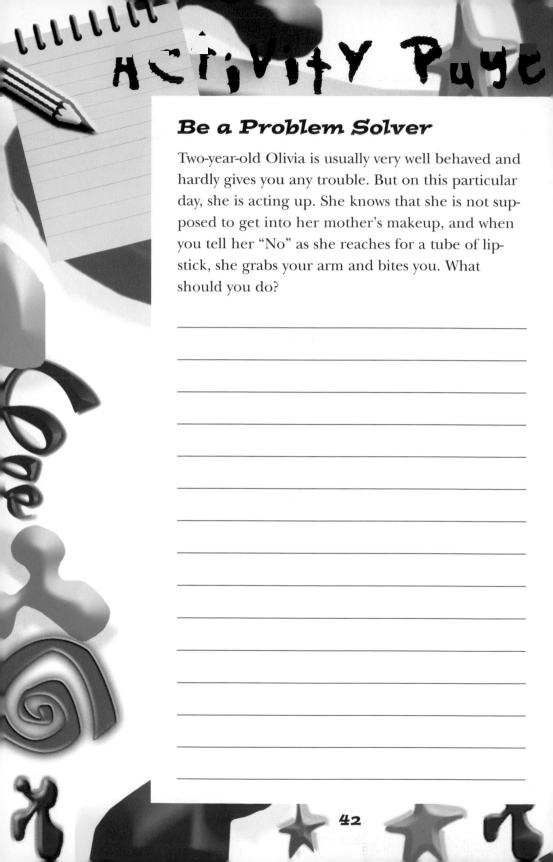

Be a Problem Solver

Two-year-old Olivia is usually very well behaved and hardly gives you any trouble. But on this particular day, she is acting up. She knows that she is not supposed to get into her mother's makeup, and when you tell her "No" as she reaches for a tube of lipstick, she grabs your arm and bites you. What should you do?

_____

_____

_____

_____

_____

_____

_____

_____

_____

_____

_____

_____

_____

_____

Eighteen-month-old Samuel just woke up from his afternoon nap. You tell him that since it's such a nice day outside, we are going to play in the backyard. As you try to help him put his pants on, he kicks his legs so that the pants fall on the floor. He seems pleased with his actions, and he runs around the room refusing to get dressed. What should you do?

Tantrums

Sometimes toddlers will yell and scream and throw themselves to the ground in anger and frustration. You can't stop them from having a tantrum. You must wait until they finish. Move any objects or furniture that might hurt them. Don't say anything. Just sit quietly until it's over. Screams will eventually shift to crying. Pat the toddler gently or stroke his or her head. When the tantrum is finished, suggest an activity to distract the toddler. Stay calm. Never shake, hit, yell at, threaten, or grab a child. Remember: Take a break, never shake!

Precautions for Toddlers

Toddlers can do a lot of things, but they don't understand danger. Watch toddlers at all times because you never know what they may do next! The best way to keep them out of trouble is to play with them and supervise them constantly.

Toddlers are at greatest danger from:

- Falls—Toddlers can walk and climb, but their balance isn't that good. They can easily fall down steps. Safety gates at the tops and bottoms of stairs could prevent these falls. Children over two may be able to climb over baby gates. Toddlers also combine their walking and climbing skills with their understanding of the world. For example, they will use the kitchen stool to climb on the counter to reach the cookies in the cupboard. They will have to pull the cupboard door hard to open it. This will knock them off balance, and they could have a nasty fall. Stay with them and anticipate possible falls.
- Swallowing objects—Toddlers can easily choke on food and toys. Keep toys with small parts or batteries out of

their reach. Always stay with them when they are eating, and make sure their food is cut up in small pieces.

- Objects in nose and ears—Toddlers may still try to put things up their nose and in their ears. You can prevent this by playing with them and watching them.
- Bumps and blows—Toddlers can't anticipate danger. They just think about the here and now. Chasing the cat is great fun until a toddler loses his or her balance and bangs his or her head against the corner of the coffee table. If a toddler's getting too wild, distract him or her with another game or activity.
- Scalds and burns—Keep toddlers safely out of your way when preparing hot drinks or meals. They may reach for a pot on the stove without knowing it's full of boiling water. They could climb up to the cookie jar and think the stove is part of the counter not knowing the burners are on.

  Also, keep hot drinks and food away from young children. Before giving food or drink to a child, make sure it is warm, but not hot. If you use a microwave oven to heat a child's food, stir it well and test the temperature before giving it to the child.

  In the bathroom, toddlers could turn on the hot water tap and burn themselves in the bath. Always stay with toddlers in the kitchen and in the bathroom.
- POISONING—Toddlers love to imitate. If they see a grown-up taking aspirin or vitamins, they might want to do the same. If you see any chemicals or other dangerous substances that haven't been stored properly, put them safely out of the toddler's reach. Tell the parents where you put them when they get home.
- Drowning—Toddlers may like the water, but they don't know how dangerous it is. If the parents have asked you to take the toddler to a wading pool or give him or her a bath, you should stay within arms reach of the child at all times. At a wading pool a toddler needs constant supervision to prevent drowning and to make sure he or she doesn't run or play dangerously. Never leave a toddler alone in or near the bath even if the phone rings. Toddlers need constant supervision to make sure they

Constantly supervise children when in or around water.

stay sitting down and play safely. They can never be safely left unattended in, on, or around water. You can learn how to provide proper supervision for toddlers in and around water through the Red Cross Assistant Lifeguard Course.

- Injuries from sharp objects—A toddler might see his father shave and later on climb up to the medicine cabinet and find that razor. Put sharp objects like razors safely out of reach. Toddlers often combine their walking, climbing, and manual skills together in creative—and sometimes dangerous—ways. Watch the toddler closely.

The thing to remember about toddlers is that they don't watch out for danger; you have to watch out for them constantly.

Toys and Games for Toddlers

Toys and games for toddlers up to two:

- Large blocks
- Cars and trucks
- Picture books
- Push and pull toys
- Play dishes
- Dolls and puppets
- Play tools
- Jack-in-the-box
- Rocking horse
- Puzzles
- Stacking blocks (knocking them down)
- Rolling a ball
- Hide-and-seek

Notes:

Matching Toy with Age

Draw lines to connect the toddler with an appropriate toy. Put an "X" over the toy that is unsafe for any age.

CHAPTER 4

Caring for Preschoolers

Stages for Preschoolers

A preschooler (three to five years) may do many or all of the following:

- Walks up and down stairs without help
- Dresses alone and puts shoes on alone
- Uses a fork and spoon
- Brushes teeth alone
- Talks well
- Asks lots of questions
- Learns to use toilet (TOILETING)
- Gains understanding of time
- Learns to ride a tricycle or a bicycle with training wheels
- Likes to show-off

Preschoolers can walk, run, talk, dress themselves, and feed themselves. They are just learning to use the toilet on their own. Preschoolers know a lot about the world and may tell you how things should be! That's why it's important that the parents explain routines and rules to you. It helps if a preschooler hears his or her parents explaining the rules to you.

Feeding

Ask the parents what foods the preschooler can eat. Remember to ask about allergies. A preschooler

may have strong ideas about the foods he or she eats. Don't argue or make a fuss. Encourage the preschooler to eat what he or she has and to try new foods. Wash his or her hands and face before and after the meal.

The parents of the preschooler you babysit may heat up foods in the microwave. Be careful when using a microwave because it can heat up foods unevenly. Stir foods well after removing them from the microwave. Always test the temperature of food and drinks by placing a little on the inside of your wrist before giving them to children.

Some preschoolers need booster seats to sit at the table. Secure the booster seat to the chair using the adjustable strap. Then place the child in the booster seat and secure the other strap around his or her waist. You may have to push the chair toward the table so the child can reach the food easily.

Most preschoolers eat with their fingers, although some will use a small fork or spoon. Eating is fun for most children. Don't worry if they are messy.

Healthy snacks for a preschooler:

- Yogurt
- Muffins
- Fresh fruit
- Plain cookies
- Juice
- Crackers
- Cheese
- Hard-boiled eggs
- Milk
- Vegetables

Activity Page

Food Find

Circle the appropriate foods for a preschooler from the selections below.

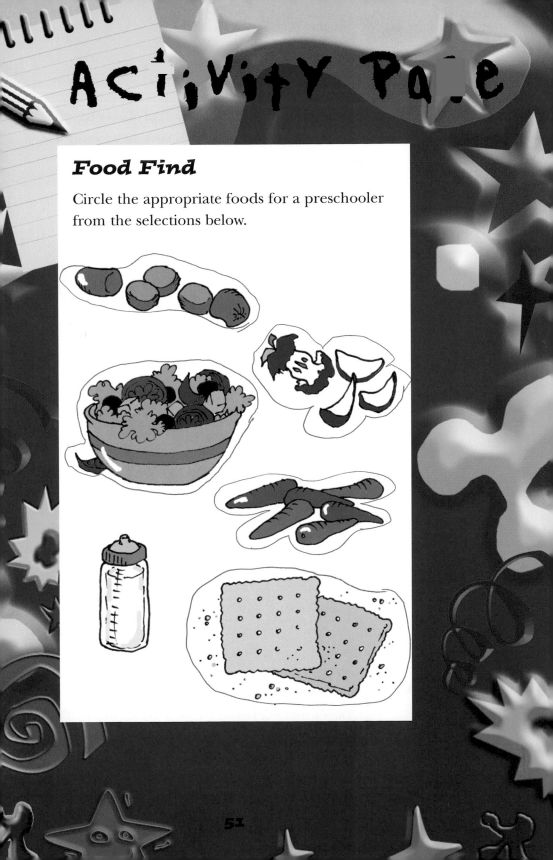

Toilet Learning

The preschooler you babysit will probably use the toilet, but he or she may need your help. Ask the parents what the toilet routine is and how the preschooler tells people he or she "has to go." Remember little girls should wipe from front to back to prevent infections.

If the child doesn't make it to the bathroom in time, there is no need to make a big deal about it. Let the child know it's okay.

Encourage the preschooler you babysit to use the toilet before you go out, before meals, and before bed. You'll probably have better luck if you say, "Okay, let's go on the toilet!" than if you ask, "Do you need to go to the toilet?" If you ask, the answer will almost always be "No."

Don't make a fuss if there is an accident. The child will probably feel bad about it. Let him or her know it's okay. Clean up and encourage the child to try again next time.

Dressing

Most preschoolers will be able to dress themselves, and they will probably have strong opinions about which outfit they want to wear. Let the child pick out the outfit he or she wants to wear sometimes or let the child choose between two outfits, but make sure it is suitable for the weather and activity that you have planned. For example, a sundress would not be appropriate for a cold, winter day!

Sleeping

It's important to know what the preschooler's bedtime routine is and what time he or she is expected to go to bed. Make sure the preschooler you babysit hears the parents explain bedtime routine and rules to you.

Give advance warning about bedtime so that the child can finish what he or she is doing and get used to the idea of bed. Don't hurry the child. Bedtime should be a quiet, relaxing time. Be firm if he or she doesn't want to go to bed and makes a fuss.

Many preschoolers will occasionally wet the bed. If this happens, don't make a big deal about it. Let him or her know it's okay. Change the child's clothes and then change the bedsheets and blankets. Be sure to tell the parents when they return what happened.

Preschoolers sometimes develop a fear of the dark or have bad dreams. If you hear the child call out in the night, go to him or her right away. Hold, comfort, reassure, and listen to the child. Stay with

him or her and gradually shift the conversation to pleasant things. When the child is calm and relaxed, tuck him or her back into bed. Explain that you are close by.

Getting Along

In your babysitting kit, pack toys and activities such as crayons and colouring books when babysitting a preschooler. Bring some old magazines and suggest a theme for a cut-and-paste collage (animals, winter, gardens, foods). Teach children how to use children's scissors safely.

Having Fun Together

Preschoolers are independent and talk well. They can be a little wild, and they still have temper tantrums from time to time.

Preschoolers love to pretend. Puzzles, dolls, guessing games, books, drawing, gluing, and play-dough, and games like follow-the-leader and hide-and-seek are usually big hits for preschoolers.

Preschoolers should spend most of their time playing and socializing, and not watching TV. If the preschooler watches TV, check with the parents about which programs are okay. The family may have a special library of videotapes/DVDs that are appropriate for the preschooler. Remember, some shows that are not scary for you may be scary for a preschooler.

Be a Problem Solver

You and three-year-old Anna are headed to the park to have some fun. Anna is having a great time on the swings, slide, and merry-go-round. After about an hour playing on the equipment, you tell Anna that it's time to go home and have lunch. Anna ignores you and runs to the see-saw. You tell her again that it's time to go, and this time she yells, "No! I don't want to go home!" What should you do?

_____

_____

_____

_____

_____

_____

_____

_____

_____

_____

_____

It's time for lunch, so you help four-year-old Colter wash his hands and climb into his booster seat at the table. You've made Colter's favourite—macaroni and cheese—but he doesn't seem to want to eat. Instead, he plays with the macaroni and is starting to make a mess. What should you do?

_____

_____

_____

_____

_____

_____

_____

_____

_____

_____

_____

_____

_____

_____

_____

Sometimes you can tell from a child's voice or body movements that he or she is getting overexcited or frustrated. This is when you should suggest a different activity. With most children, you can anticipate problems and avoid them before they arise.

As a last resort, a preschooler may at times need a "time out" to give him or her a chance to calm down and cool off after a frustrating event. Do not isolate the child. Be caring and explain other positive ways to behave. After time out is over, give a hug and move on to another activity.

Preschoolers like to say "No" so remember, no open-ended questions. Offer choices very carefully. Don't ask, "Do you want milk?" Ask, "Do you want your milk in the red cup or the green cup?"

Precautions for Preschoolers

You need to know where the preschooler you babysit is allowed to play and which areas of the house are off-limits. Preschoolers are noisy, so silence often means trouble. If it ever seems too quiet: Check it out!

Preschoolers also have a lot of opinions about how things should go. They might say something like, "My daddy always lets me climb this tree." This may be true, but if the father hasn't told you that and you think the child may get hurt, put safety first and ask him or her to get down and offer another game to play.

Preschoolers are at the greatest danger from:

- Falls—Most preschoolers love the playground and like to climb. If he or she is not careful or moves too quickly, he or she can easily lose his or her balance and fall. Watch the child carefully. If he or she is getting too wild, offer a distraction like another game or activity.
- Play mishap—Preschoolers have the ability to hurt themselves in any number of ways while they are playing. They could be playing "telephone booth" and try and put a coin into an electrical outlet. They could pretend to be a ghost and put a plastic bag over the head. This could be a suffocation hazard. Plastic bags should be kept out of children's reach. While playing hide and seek, preschoolers may hide in trunks or a cupboard where they cannot breathe. If you play with the children you can prevent these injuries.

- Poisoning—A preschooler might be in the middle of a pretend game of hospital. He or she might want some cough syrup to get better and might get some from the medicine cabinet and drink some. Make sure all dangerous chemicals and medicines are stored properly out of children's reach.

- Drowning—A preschooler you babysit may be learning to swim and loves the water. Because of his or her confidence and ability, it's easy to turn your head and think about something else. During this time, the child could get into the water over his or her head. Do not go swimming with a preschooler if there is no lifeguard or adult present to provide additional safety supervision. Never take your eyes off a child in the water! You should stay within arm's reach of the child in, on, or around the water at all times.

Supervision (by staying with them) is the key to keeping the children you babysit safe.

- Swallowing objects—Preschoolers still love to put things in their mouth. They could use small things like marbles to play a game where they count how many marbles fit in their mouth. Preschoolers should not be allowed to play with marbles; these could choke them.

Toys and Games for Preschoolers

Toys and games for preschoolers:

- Dolls and trucks
- Paper and crayons
- Picture books
- Painting
- Balls
- Sand toys
- Toy dishes
- Toy broom
- Playdough
- Dress-up
- Playing outside
- Blowing soap bubbles

Notes:

_____

_____

Matching Toy with Age

Draw lines to connect the pre-schooler with an appropriate toy. Put an "X" over the toy that is unsafe for any age.

Caring for School-Aged Children

Stages for School-Aged Children

A school-aged child (five years and older) may do many or all of the following:

- Understands games that have rules
- Knows what is pretend and what is real
- Does more by him- or herself
- Is interested in sports and music

School-aged children are used to being around people. They admire "big kids" and teenagers. If you show an interest in them and what they like to do, they'll probably become your good friend.

Feeding

Find out from the parents of the school-aged child you babysit what the rules about snacks and meals are. When should he or she eat? What foods are okay? What foods are off limits? Does the child have any allergies?

Choose healthy foods for mealtime. Canada's Food Guide to Healthy Eating recommends choosing foods from the four colours of the rainbow—grains, vegetables and fruits, milk products, and meat and alternatives. Make healthy foods fun by cutting sandwiches into circles or triangles and fixing "ants on a log" (celery sticks with peanut butter and raisins; use cream cheese for children with peanut allergies). Snacks are a great way to refuel. Choose snacks from different food groups—a glass of milk and a few graham crackers, yogurt, or some dry cereal.

The school-aged child you babysit should hear his or her parents explain rules and routines to you so there are no conflicts later ("My mom always lets me eat ice cream for a snack!").

School-aged children like being treated like big kids. Get them to help at meals. They can set the table, help make sandwiches, and pour milk.

Notes:

_____

_____

_____

_____

_____

_____

_____

_____

Food Find

Circle the appropriate foods for a school-aged child from the selections below.

Bedtime

Make sure you know the routine of the school-aged child you babysit! How many stories? Does he or she get a glass of water? What if he or she wakes up?

Be firm if the child doesn't want to stay in bed. If the child says, "I can't sleep," let him or her look at books or play quietly in bed for 10 minutes. Tell the child that when the 10 minutes are up, it's time to sleep.

Getting Along

The best way to get along with children is to be positive. If you keep kids busy and happy, you will enjoy the time you spend together.

Good impressions are important. Try to get things off to a good start. Be friendly and interested in the children without being "gushy." For example,

before bedtime instead of saying, "You have to turn off the TV and go to bed now," try, "Now it's time for stories before bed. Would you like to pick the stories from your bookshelf or do you want to look at the ones I've brought? Let's get your teeth done and pajamas on, then we'll be ready to read."

If a problem arises, stay positive and find a way to cooperate so everybody feels like a winner. Try not to dwell on the negative. Be consistent, and mean what you say. Avoid making threats or promises. Always be firm about safety rules!

The school-aged child you babysit probably has some well-established interests. Try to find out ahead of time what they are. If he or she has a card collection, bring a few that you may have. Pack some board games and card games in your babysitter's kit. They are also popular for this age group.

Having Fun Together

Talk with the school-aged child you babysit about what it is he or she is most interested in and go from there. If he or she tells you he has a bug collection, ask to see it, and if appropriate, go for a walk to collect some more.

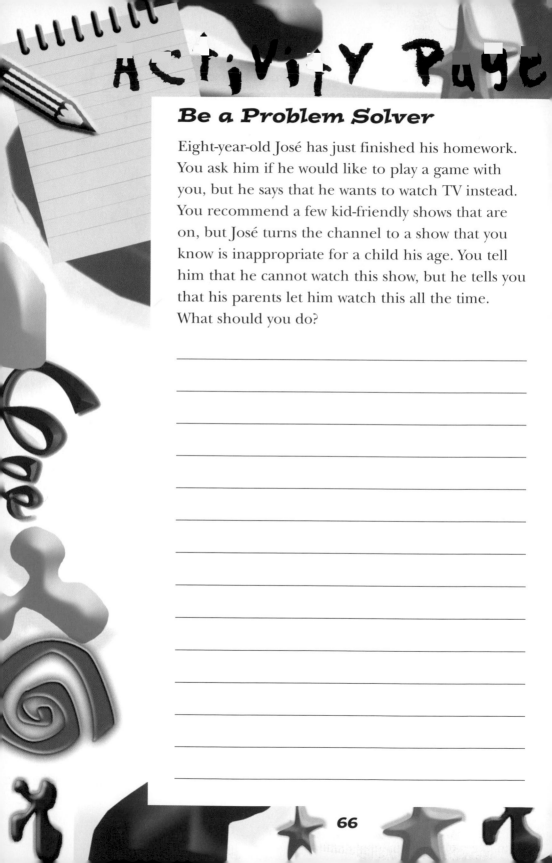

ActiViTy PaGe

Be a Problem Solver

Eight-year-old José has just finished his homework. You ask him if he would like to play a game with you, but he says that he wants to watch TV instead. You recommend a few kid-friendly shows that are on, but José turns the channel to a show that you know is inappropriate for a child his age. You tell him that he cannot watch this show, but he tells you that his parents let him watch this all the time. What should you do?

_____

_____

_____

_____

_____

_____

_____

_____

_____

_____

_____

_____

_____

Your parents have asked you to watch your little sister Phuong while they go to the theatre. They've asked you to make sure that Phuong cleans her room, since she didn't do it the night before and it's a mess. Phuong has been in her room for 15 minutes, so you check on her to see how the cleaning is coming along. When you open her bedroom door, you see that her room is still a mess and she's lying on her bed reading. You tell her again that she needs to start cleaning up, but she replies, "You can't tell me what to do! You're not Mom, you know!" What should you do?

_____

_____

_____

_____

_____

_____

_____

_____

_____

_____

_____

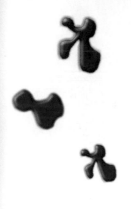

School-aged children think "big kids" are neat, and if you show an interest in what the child you babysit likes doing, you'll probably have a pretty cooperative kid to look after.

School-aged children are big enough to know the routines and rules. If the child you babysit gives you trouble, he or she can have some "time out." After time out ask him or her to join you for a game. Let the incident be forgotten.

Precautions for School-Aged Children

If you think there may be danger, put safety first and say "No." Remember, you're the one in charge!

School-aged children may like to show off a little bit. They are capable and independent and have confidence in their abilities. The school-aged child you babysit knows the household rules and might tell you that he or she is allowed to ride the bike to the corner store. Once again, if you haven't been told this by the parents, then you should say "No." Tell the child that you'll check with the parents for the next time.

School-aged children are at greatest danger from:

- Burns—Make sure the school-aged child does not play with matches or lighters because they can get burned.
- Car-related injuries—The school-aged child you babysit might often play unsupervised in front of his or her house with friends. He or she may know about street safety, but needs to be reminded. The child could be so wrapped in a game that a car coming down the street could go unnoticed. If the child you babysit wants to go outside and play with friends, go along and watch. Ask the parents about the household rules for playing outside; for example, how far from the house is the child allowed to go on his or her own?

- Bicycle-related injuries—The school-aged child you babysit probably knows how to ride a bicycle safely and knows that wearing a helmet is a must. Ask the parents about the household rules for cycling, for example, where the child is allowed to ride or whether or not you need to be right with him or her all the time.

  Sometimes, especially if friends are around, the child may forget about riding safely. Before going cycling, review the safety rules with him or her. If the child is riding unsafely, suggest another game or activity.

- Drowning—If the school-aged child you babysit can swim, he or she may like playing in the water. Be aware that drowning can occur suddenly. So never take children near water if there is no lifeguard on duty or you don't have another adult assisting you in supervising the children. You can learn how to perform safe rescues by taking Red Cross Swim Kids lessons. Review and follow the water safety rules (staying in shallow water, but never diving in shallow water) and stay with him or her at all times. Ask the parents whether the child is allowed to swim as long as you are supervising closely; ask the parents how well the child can swim and what the household rules are for swimming in this location (e.g., the pool or beach). If you don't feel comfortable giving children your full attention, you should refuse to babysit around water.

Toys and Games for School-Aged Children

School-aged children have specific interests and favourite things to do. Ask the child you are babysitting what he or she likes to do, who his or her friends are, and about other interests. Really listen and show an interest. The child may also like playing board games or cards. Magic tricks, joke books, and riddles may also be a big hit.

Activity Page

Matching Toy with Age

Draw lines to connect the school-aged child with an appropriate toy. Put an "X" over the toy that is unsafe for any age.

True-or-False Brain Teaser

Based on what you've already learned, decide which of these statements are true and which are false by marking a T (true) or F (false) beside them. For each false statement, change the statement so that it becomes true.

EXAMPLE

Not All children of the same age like the same things. *F*

1. Shaking a baby is okay as a last resort. *F*

2. Before a child goes to sleep, it's a good idea to do an exciting activity, like a game of tag. *F*

3. Put a baby face down to sleep. *F*

4. When heating foods in the microwave, always test the temperature before giving the food to a child. *T*

5. When a toddler has a toilet learning "accident," make a fuss about it so he or she will learn not to do it again. *F*

6. Since you're in charge, don't bother asking the parents about any rules or routines. *F*

7. Babies can play with any type of toy as long as you are nearby. *F*

8. The biggest responsibility a babysitter has is to keep the children safe. *T*

9. There is only one type of diaper—disposable. *F*

10. Ask children often if they need to go to the bathroom. *F*

11. When changing a girl's diaper, always wipe from the front to the back to prevent infection. *T*

Summary of Decision-Making Abilities

You have learned about providing care for babies, toddlers, preschoolers, and school-aged children. They are at different ages and developmental stages and have different needs. You have also learned to solve problems that may occur while you are babysitting by using leadership and decision-making skills. By using what you learn in this course and the information in this manual, you can be confident in your ability to babysit children of different ages and make good decisions. You're on your way to becoming a great babysitter!

Notes:

_____

_____

_____

_____

_____

_____

_____

_____

_____

CHAPTER 6

Injury Is No Accident: Creating Safe Environments

Home Safety

Did you know thousands of children are seen in hospital emergency departments each year in Canada? For children under 10, home is the most common place for injury. Most of these injuries happen to children under the age of five. The main causes of death in the home are fires, falls, poisoning, choking, suffocation, and drowning.

Home safety is about creating a safe environment for the children you are babysitting. You are on the front line in the prevention of such injuries. Babysitters must anticipate and avoid them—injuries can be prevented!

In the Kitchen
- Use back burners as much as possible. Turn pan handles inside toward the back of the stove.
- Keep children away from the stove, kettles, ovens, hot taps, heaters, matches, and cigarette lighters.
- Keep hot drinks and hot food away from young children.
- Make sure electrical outlets are covered. Electrical wires should be safely out of reach and sight.

73

- Store all sharp objects out of reach.
- Make sure all cleaning products and medicines, including vitamins, are out of reach.

On the Phone

- When you answer the phone while babysitting, say that the parents are busy and can't come to the phone. Offer to take a message.
- Don't say you are the babysitter or that the parents are out, if someone asks "What number is this?" Instead, answer, "What number did you dial?" Don't give out the number of where you are. Don't say what time the parents will be available.
- If someone insists on speaking with the parents, take a message and call the parents to relay the message.
- If a caller is aggressive or threatening, hang up. Phone the police, the parents, the neighbour whose number you've been given, and then call your parents.

Visits

- Look through a window or a peephole to see who is knocking at the door. Open the door only to people you know who have permission from the parents to come in. If a visitor is expected, get a description from the parents.
- Talk to strangers through a window or a chained door. Say the parents are busy and can't come to the door. Offer to take a message or don't answer the door at all.
- If a stranger is aggressive and won't leave, call the police, the parents, the neighbour whose number you've been given, and then call your parents. Don't go outside.
- Close the drapes or blinds when it's dark outside.

Make sure emergency numbers are posted by the phones.

Outdoor Play Safety
On the Street

Constantly supervise children when they are outdoors. Make sure the children walk on the sidewalk near you or are holding your hand. Insist on stopping and looking carefully before crossing the street.

At the Park

Look around and make sure it is a safe place:

- Is there any broken glass or sharp objects?
- Are there any stray dogs?
- Is the playground equipment safe?
- Are there any strangers that make you uneasy?
- Are there other people in the park that could assist you if you needed help?

Young children are safer on play equipment that is smaller or lower to the ground. For toddlers and preschoolers, stay close enough to catch them if they are climbing or sliding.

Supervise Play

Make sure the children's clothing is safe. Check that loose scarves, drawstrings, and mitten strings have been removed when children play on playground equipment to reduce the potential for strangulation.

Make sure the children play safely and use age-appropriate equipment. Watch them at all times. If any strangers approach who make you feel at all uneasy, leave the park immediately.

Bicycle Safety

All children on bicycles and tricycles should wear helmets! (Including you.)

Be outside with the children when they are riding their tricycles or bicycles. You are the traffic controller! If the child you are babysitting rides a tricycle, make sure he or she is wearing a helmet and rides safely on the sidewalk or on a hard surface at the park.

Ask parents how well the child can ride a bicycle and about the household rules for cycling. Make sure the school-aged child you babysit wears a bicycle helmet, and to obey the rules of the road:

- always ride single-file;
- use a bike lane if possible; if not, ride in the same direction as the cars;
- always ride as close to the curb as possible.

Check out your surroundings when you are outside, and watch children at all times.

Fire Safety

In addition to emergency information that you should have next to the phone, make sure you know the layout of the house. You should know what the fire escape routes are and the outside meeting place.

Fire can spread very quickly. In case of fire get everyone out of the house first! Your first priority is to get all occupants out of the house as quickly as possible. Don't stop to pick up anything else. Call 9-1-1 or the local fire department from a neighbour's house. Then call the parents.

- Never go back into the house to get anything.
- If you are upstairs and fire is coming up the stairs, move to the room farthest from the fire.
- Close all the doors between you and the fire. Always touch a door before opening it. If the door is hot, do not open it. Shout or telephone for help.
- If there is a small fire on the stove or in the oven, smother the flames by closing the oven door or covering the pot with a metal lid. Use a fire extinguisher if possible. If the fire is big, get the children out of the house and call for help.
- If clothes are on fire remember to "Stop, Drop, and Roll." Stop immediately where you are. Drop to the ground. Roll over and over. Cover your face and mouth with your hands to protect yourself and your breathing. Roll over and over until the flames are out. Don't allow a child to run. Smother the flames in a blanket or coat or by rolling the child on the ground.
- Never smoke while you are babysitting. Careless smoking is the leading cause of fire.

Water Safety

Drowning is a leading cause of injury and death of children. Know your limits! You must be ready to watch the children constantly if they are near water. If you don't feel comfortable giving children your undivided attention while they are near the water, and if you do not know how to perform safe rescues, you should refuse to babysit around water. Never take a baby or child swimming without the parents' permission, and plan on getting in the water with them. Be aware that babies and children get cold quickly and guard closely against the chills.

Babies and Toddlers up to Three

Never take your eyes off babies or toddlers when they are in or around water. Wading pools and baths should be emptied if they're not being used. Toddlers and babies are very unstable walking in water and lose their balance easily. They also have limited depth perception. They may drop a toy into a pool and try to reach it, even if it is in deep water. They may fall in the water trying. Even a few inches of water is enough to drown a small baby or toddler!

Preschoolers

Make sure the preschooler you babysit only goes in the shallow water with your permission and that you go in the water with the child. You both must stay in shallow water. No horseplay! Walk, don't run, at the side of the pool. One child at a time on a slide. All children near water need constant, direct supervision. You should stay within arm's reach of the child in the water at all times!

School-Aged Children

The school-aged child you babysit may be a good swimmer and may show off. Ask the parents how well the child can swim and what are the household rules for swimming. Make sure he or she only goes in the water with your permission and when a lifeguard or another adult is supervising, and understands safety rules about running and horseplay. All children near water need constant, direct supervision. Swim in supervised areas only.

Personal Safety and Security

Staying safe and creating a safe environment means more than just preventing and managing injuries. It also means being and feeling secure. All children have a right to be respected and protected from harm. The children you babysit need to know they can trust you and depend on you to provide that protection and respect.

Keep your first aid kit handy but out of the children's reach.

Dealing with Strangers

A stranger is anyone you and the children do not know well. You will probably meet strangers from time to time. People you don't know may come to the door, or may speak to you when you are at the park or in the neighbourhood.

Strangers may be friendly and there may not be an intent to hurt you in any way. However, you cannot take chances. The fact that you don't know a stranger means you can't tell what he or she is like or what the person wants. You have to watch out for the children, and yourself, at all times.

Never go, or allow the children to go, anywhere with a stranger, for any reason. Never put yourself or the children in a position where they could be taken away by a stranger. Stay where there are a lot of other people around. Always watch the children. Never go toward a stranger in or near a car or van.

Trust your instincts. If anyone or anything makes you feel uncomfortable or nervous, find an adult you know and can trust. If a stranger bothers you when you aren't near anyone else you know, walk away. If you have to, yell or scream to attract attention. Don't be afraid to call for help.

Rural Babysitting

What if someone living more than 10 km out of town asks you to babysit? What do you need to know to keep you and the children you babysit safe?

Think safety whether you are inside the house or out in the yard. Childproofing a house is the same in the country as in town, but outside there are differences. Rural areas, for example, won't have busy streets you may have to try and cross safely, but there will be a driveway and a country road that may have huge farm machinery and equipment to avoid.

As part of your safety checklist, review with the parents the safe areas for playing and the absolute off-limits areas. It's a good idea for you, the parents, and children to walk the farm or propety so that everyone knows where it is safe to play and what must be avoided. Some parents may even have a risk map prepared for you. Remember to always enforce the off-limits areas:

- Avoid farm equipment and machinery.
- Stay away from grain bins/wagons/trucks and flowing grain.
- Don't touch chemicals or hazardous products (know the labels), guns, or matches.
- Respect livestock animals, always keeping a fence between children and animals.
- Avoid dugouts, sloughs, silage pits, and manure pits.

Know the safety and emergency procedures and the back-up plan developed by you and the hiring parents. It will help you feel comfortable and confident on the job. As part of the emergency procedures, make sure the parents write down the correct address and specific directions so that you can provide clear instructions if you have to call for help. If possible, carry a cell phone so you can call for help at any time. Always carry emergency phone numbers whenever you and the children are outdoors.

Keep in mind that when babysitting in a rural location, neighbours, or other people, will not be nearby. Help will take longer to arrive because of the distance.

Wearing a small waist pack with a cell phone and emergency numbers, a few first aid supplies, and a flashlight will help you be prepared.

Notes:

_____

_____

_____

_____

_____

_____

_____

Notes:

Safety Search

Look for safety-related problems in the house and the yard on p. 83. Using a highlighter, colour the problems you find, and then list the problems and how you would fix the problems in the columns on this page.

What's the Problem?	How to Fix It

CHAPTER 7

How to Handle Emergencies and First Aid

Handling Emergencies

The most important part of being a babysitter is making sure the children in your care are safe.

With your training and good judgment, you'll know how to prevent injuries and illnesses.

Preventing Injury and Illness

Remember:

- *Recognize* the safety-related problem (e.g., check the home for potential hazards).
- *Remove* the safety-related problem if it is safe to do so (e.g., pick up small objects from the floor that could cause a baby to choke).
- *Limit* the safety-related problem if you can't remove it (e.g., give children safe and real choices).
- *Give care* if an emergency does occur (e.g., give first aid care).

But what if a serious injury does occur? What do you do?

This section will help you gain skills and confidence so that you can respond to an emergency. This is not a first aid course, remember to stay calm and you should only treat an injury to the best of your ability. Always get help if you need it. Always inform parents of any injury.

If you have already taken a first aid course, the information that follows will help remind you of emergency procedures. If you have not taken a first aid course, the procedures that follow are for information only. We strongly encourage babysitters to take a Canadian Red Cross First Aid & CPR course.

How to Call for Help

What is EMS?

The Emergency Medical Services (EMS) System is the network that gets injured people to hospitals as quickly as possible. The person who calls EMS begins a chain reaction that includes the **DISPATCHER** who answers the phone and the EMS professional who arrives at the scene of the emergency (police, firefighters, ambulance, or medical attendants).

Emergency Phone Numbers:

_____

_____

Poison Control Centre:

1800-268-9017

You are the first part of the EMS chain when you call 9-1-1 or the appropriate number for your community.

Addresses (location of babysitting job):

_____

_____

When Should I Call EMS?

You should call EMS/9-1-1 if you see anyone who is:

- UNCONSCIOUS
- Not breathing (no coughing, no movement) or having difficulty breathing
- Bleeding a lot
- Vomiting blood or has blood in his or her urine
- Poisoned

or see anyone who has:

- **SEIZURES,** severe headache, or slurred speech
- Broken bones
- Head or spine injuries

Use your common sense about calling EMS/9-1-1. If you think there is an emergency, there probably is. Call EMS/9-1-1 before calling parents or your family.

How Do I Call EMS?

1. If you can, send a responsible person to call EMS, while you provide care.

2. Tell the caller to phone 9-1-1. If your community does not have 9-1-1 services, the phone number for emergencies should be posted by the phone. Otherwise dial "O" for the operator to get the local emergency number or to be transferred to the appropriate agency.

3. Tell the caller what the dispatcher needs to know:

- Where the emergency is. You should give the exact address and include the name of the city or town.
- What the cross streets are. Describe any landmarks, the name of the building, the floor, and room number.

- The telephone number from where the call is being made. This way EMS can call back if necessary.
- The caller's name.
- What has happened (car-related injuries, fall, fire).
- How many people are injured.
- The condition of the injured person or people (CONSCIOUS or unconscious, breathing, bleeding, etc.). The dispatcher will ask the age of the injured person.
- The first aid being given.

4. Tell the caller not to hang up the phone until the dispatcher hangs up.

5. Also, tell the caller to come back to where you are and tell you what the dispatcher said.

If you are alone with an injured person, shout "Help!" You may attract someone who can help you by making the call. If no one comes, get to a phone as fast as you can to call EMS/9-1-1. Then go back to the injured person to give care.

What to Do in an Emergency

Whenever you think an emergency has occurred, follow the emergency action steps (CHECK, CALL, CARE). They'll help you help others as quickly and as safely as possible.

CHECK

1. Check the scene first.

2. Look around for clues that show what happened. Make sure the area is safe before you give care.

3. Make sure there is nothing that could hurt you or cause further harm to the baby or child. Use DISPOS-ABLE GLOVES when you might touch any body fluids.

CHECK

1. Check the baby or child.

2. See if the baby or child responds. Ask the child, "Are you okay?" or clap loudly and gently flick the bottom of the baby's feet or tap the child on the shoulder to see if she or he is awake and breathing.

CALL

Call EMS/9-1-1 if there is no response. Send someone to make the call. If you are trained in Child CPR, do five cycles (two minutes) of CPR, then go call.

CARE

1. The care you give depends on the kind of emergency. Use the first aid tips in the next section when giving care.

2. Don't move the injured child unless the child is in danger where he or she is.

3. Help the child rest in a comfortable position and reassure him or her.

Illness

You should call parents right away if the child you are babysitting seems sick. Signs of illness are:

- Constant crying
- Fever (feeling hot to the touch)
- Having a hard time breathing
- Pain
- Vomiting
- Dizziness for more than a few seconds

Choking
Prevention

- Careful, slow eating and chewing of food.
- No walking, running, laughing, or talking while eating.
- Make sure objects such as pen caps or coins aren't in children's mouths.
- Keep the children still when they have food in their hands and mouths.
- Feed babies and young children soft foods in small pieces. Stay with them while they eat.
- Always check the environment to make sure no small toys or objects are near babies or children who put things in their mouths.
- Keep young children away from balloons that can pop into small pieces and be easily inhaled.

For Babies up to One year

CHOKING (CONSCIOUS)

You see the baby you are babysitting coughing or breathing forcefully.

☺ CHECK

the scene and the baby.

1. If the baby can breathe or cough, stay with him or her. Don't try to stop the baby from coughing. Don't slap the baby on the back.
2. If the baby is making high-pitched noises, wheezing, can no longer make a sound, or becomes too weak to cough:

☎ CALL

1. Shout for help.
2. Send someone to call EMS/9-1-1.

🖐 CARE

1. Hold the baby face down on your arm between your hand and your elbow. The baby's head should be lower than the body.
2. Hold the baby's jaw firmly. Rest your arm on your thigh.
3. With the heel of your hand, give five firm back blows between the shoulder blades.

4. If the baby is still choking, turn his or her face upon your thigh with the head lower than the body. Hold the back of the head.
5. Imagine a line between the baby's nipples. Place two fingers on the centre of the breastbone one finger width below the imaginary line.
6. With your two fingers, push down five times (these are called chest thrusts). You should press down $1/3$ to $1/2$ the depth of the chest. Match your strength to the baby's size.

(continued)

CHOKING (Conscious)

7. After five chest thrusts do five more firm back blows.

8. Repeat the chest thrusts and back blows sequence until:
- The object comes out
- The baby starts crying, breathing, or coughing forcefully
- The baby becomes unconscious

9. If the baby becomes unconscious, call EMS/9-1-1 for help if you have not already called.

For Children Over One

Choking (Conscious)

You see the child you are babysitting coughing or breathing forcefully.

☺ CHECK

the scene and the child.

1. Help the child lean forward. Encourage him or her to cough. Stay with the child. Don't slap him or her on the back.

2. If the child's face is turning blue and he or she is making a whistling sound:

☎ CALL

1. Shout for help.

2. Send someone to call EMS/9-1-1.

✋ CARE

1. Stand behind the child (for a small child you may need to kneel behind him or her) and provide support by placing one arm diagonally across the chest and then bend the child forward at the waist. Give five firm back blows between the shoulder blades with the heel of one hand.

2. If the object has not come out of the child's mouth, put your arms around the waist. Make a tight fist. Put it just above his or her belly button with your thumb against the belly.

3. Put your other hand over your fist.

4. Press your fist into the child's belly with a quick, inward and upward thrust. Do this five times.

5. Match your strength to the child's size. The smaller the child, the gentler the thrusts.

6. After five abdominal thrusts, do five more firm back blows.

7. Repeat the cycle of abdominal thrusts and back blows until:

   • The object comes out
   • The child starts breathing or coughing forcefully
   • The child becomes unconscious

8. If the child becomes unconscious, call EMS/9-1-1 for help if you have not already called.

Notes:

Bleeding
Cuts and Wounds

For a very serious **CUT** with lots of bleeding, remember:

Rest. Have the child sit or lie down.

Direct Pressure. Use a clean cloth applied directly over the cut.

Remember: Use disposable gloves when you might touch any body fluids.

😊 CHECK

the scene and the child.

The child's hand has a bad cut.

☎ CALL

Call EMS/9-1-1 if:

- Bleeding does not stop within a few minutes.
- Blood is spurting from the **WOUND**.
- The wound is on the stomach, the chest, or a joint.
- You can see muscle or bone inside the wound.
- The wound is longer than 2.5 cm (1 in) or is deep.
- The wound has an object stuck in it.

✋ CARE

1. Hold a clean cloth firmly against the wound. Remember to wear disposable gloves.

2. Get help if there is a lot of bleeding. Call EMS/9-1-1.

3. Have the child lie down and stay still.

4. If the cloth you are using soaks through, don't take it away. Put another cloth over it.

5. Tie a bandage around the cloth. If the cut is on the child's neck, don't tie a bandage on, just hold the cloth firmly.

6. If the bleeding stops, make a sling, or use bandages to keep the hand from moving.

7. If the skin below the wound tingles, is cold or blue, the bandage is too tight. Loosen it slightly. If colour or temperature does not improve, call EMS/ 9-1-1.

8. Wash your hands as soon as possible.

Scrapes

The child you are babysitting falls and scrapes a knee.

1. Wash the SCRAPE with running water for 5 minutes.

2. Wash the skin around the scrape with soap and water. Rinse off the soap thoroughly.

3. Blot the scrape with a STERILE, gauze dressing from the first aid kit, or the medicine cabinet.

4. Cover with a sterile bandage.

Impaled Object

The child you are babysitting has a piece of glass sticking out of a leg or arm.

Don't try to take it out. Never remove an impaled object; it might cause SEVERE BLEEDING.

1. Cut any clothing away from the object.

2. Put bulky bandages around the object to keep it from moving.

3. Tie the bandages in place.

4. Get help right away.

If the child has a splinter sticking out of the skin, it is okay to use tweezers to remove it. Pull out the splinter at the same angle that it went into the skin.

Nose Bleeds

The child you are babysitting has a nose bleed.

1. Tell the child to sit down; try to get him or her to relax.

2. Tilt his or her head forward a little bit.

3. Pinch the nostrils firmly together.

4. Hold firmly for at least 10 minutes without letting go.

5. If bleeding continues, get help right away.

Internal Bleeding

The child you are babysitting falls off a play structure at the park. He or she may have internal bleeding if he or she has these signs:

- Very thirsty
- Pain where he or she was hurt
- Yawning and gasping for air
- Faintness
- Red or black vomit
- Bright foamy blood coughed up
- Swelling where he or she was hurt

Don't lift the child's feet. Don't give him or her anything to drink. Don't move the child if you think he or she has hurt his or her head or neck, unless he or she is having a hard time breathing.

1. If the child has a hard time breathing because he or she is bleeding from the nose, mouth, or ears, roll him or her on the side.

2. Send someone to call EMS/9-1-1.

Sprains, Strains, and Fractures

CHECK the scene and the baby or child.

CALL EMS/9-1-1 if:

- You think a child has injured his or her head, neck, or back
- The injury makes walking or breathing difficult
- You think there are several injuries

CARE

For common injuries remember RICE:

R – rest. Make the child as comfortable as possible.

I – immobilize. Immobilizing the injury lessens pain, prevents further damage, and reduces the risk of bleeding.

C – cold. Cold reduces pain and swelling.

E – elevate. Raising the injury reduces swelling.

Children can hurt their heads from a fall of only 15 cm (6 in).

Signs of head injury are:

- Headache
- Dizziness or disorientation
- **NAUSEA** or vomiting
- Loss of consciousness
- Bleeding or clear liquid from ear or nose

Signs of neck and back injuries are:

- Pain
- Loss of feeling
- Loss of strength

Signs of arm or leg injuries are:

- Pain
- Tenderness
- Swelling

A head injury may also mean a neck or back injury. Do not move the child unless he or she is in a dangerous place.

A child has fallen off a swing at the park and seems to be hurt.

CHECK the scene and the child.

Check if he or she is conscious. Ask, "Are you okay?"

CALL

If he or she doesn't answer, shout for help. Have someone call EMS/9-1-1, or if you are alone, call yourself.

CARE

1. If the child is not breathing, begin child CPR if you are trained to do so.

2. If the child is breathing but is unconscious, check for blood, vomit, or noisy breathing. If there is none, don't move the child.

3. If you hear gurgling, noisy breathing, or see fluid from the nose or mouth, roll the child onto the side to help the child breathe better. Let the upper arm and leg roll toward the ground in the RECOVERY POSITION. Try to turn the child's body all at the same time so that the neck is not twisted.

4. Check to see whether the child is wearing a MedicAlert® bracelet or necklace.

Poison

Prevention

- Keep children away from all medications, cleaning products, and poisonous plants. Consider all household or drugstore products potentially harmful, including multi-vitamins and headache and cold medication.
- Never call medicine "candy" to try to get a child to take it.
- Never store household products in a food or drink container.
- Make sure the Poison Control Centre number is near the telephone.
- Wear shoes outdoors. Don't walk through high grass or bushes.

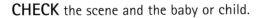

CHECK the scene and the baby or child.

CALL

If you suspect any type of poisoning, call the local Poison Control Centre number (#_____) immediately to get advice. This telephone number should be posted with other emergency phone numbers.

CARE

Care for life-threatening conditions first. Provide care according to instructions from the Poison Control Centre or EMS/9-1-1 dispatcher.

Poisonings can happen in different ways.

Inhaled Poison

Signs of inhaled poison are:

- Red, sore eyes, nose, or throat
- Coughing, hard time breathing, dizziness
- Vomiting, seizures
- Bluish colour around the mouth or red face
- Unconsciousness

Note: For inhaled poisons move the child to fresh air immediately. Call EMS/9-1-1.

Poison on the Skin

Signs of poison on the skin:

- Burning, itching, swelling, blisters
- Headache, fever

Swallowed Poison

Signs of a swallowed chemical:

- Burning in the mouth, throat, or stomach
- Cramps, gagging, diarrhea, nausea, vomiting

Signs of a swallowed plant or drug:

- Vomiting, seizures
- Irregular pulse
- Drowsiness, having a hard time talking
- Lack of coordination
- Dizziness
- Rapid breathing

Burns

Prevention

- Keep matches and lighters away from children. Always supervise children.
- Do not hold a hot drink while carrying a baby. Keep hot drinks and food where children cannot reach them.
- Cook on the stove with pot handles turned in. Use rear burners. Keep children away from the stove area.
- Never put water on a grease fire.
- Do not spray aerosol cans near an open fire.
- Never use electrical appliances near water.
- Cover electrical outlets with safety caps.
- Avoid the sun between 10:00 A.M. and 3:00 P.M.
- Wear protective clothing from the sun (including hats).
- Use a sunscreen.

CHECK the scene and the child.

CALL EMS/9-1-1 for burns that:
- involve difficulty breathing
- cover more than one body part
- occur on the head, neck, hands, feet, or genitals
- result from chemicals, explosions, or electricity
- are deep (skin has blisters or looks brown or black)

CARE for the child.

Chemical Burns

The child you are babysitting has an area of red skin and is crying. You think the child might have played with some cleaning products.

1. Rinse the affected skin with cold water for 15 minutes. Don't use ice. Use a shower or hose if you need to.

2. Take off any clothing that got the chemical on it while you are rinsing.

3. Cover the burned skin with a clean, dry, nonstick dressing.

4. Get help right away and call EMS/9-1-1.

Heat Burns

The child you are babysitting has been playing near a hot radiator and has burned his or her leg.

Don't take off any clothing that may be stuck to the burn. If there are any blisters, leave them alone.

Never put greasy ointments, butter, lotions, or creams on burns.

1. Put the burned skin in cool water for at least 15 minutes. Don't use ice.

2. Cover with a clean, dry, nonstick dressing.

3. Get help for burns that are more than 5 cm (2 in) around and for burns that are blistered, white, or black. Call EMS/9-1-1 for all burns to the head, neck, hands, feet, or genitals.

Electrical Burns

You hear a sudden loud pop from the bedroom of a child you are babysitting. You see a lamp overturned. The child seems confused and his or her hand is burned. The child is having difficulty breathing.

1. Make sure the area is safe and there is no further risk of shock.

2. Monitor the child's breathing.

3. Look for two burns: where the electrical current entered and exited. They are often on hands or feet.

4. Cover the burns with a clean, dry, nonstick dressing.

5. Call EMS/9-1-1 for help.

Special Health Problems

You should find out what special health problems the children you are looking after have. If they have any special needs or problems, you need to know how to avoid problems and what to do if the children get sick.

Allergies

One in five children in North America has some kind of **ALLERGY**. The most common allergies are to tree and grass pollens, dust, insect bites, food, and medications. Always ask the parents if the children you are caring for have allergies. Some children may carry an EpiPen® in a special kit. Find out what you should do to assist if there is a problem. The child may have learned to take their own medication. You may need to know where to get it or how to get it ready for them.

Signs of allergic reaction:

- Rash, hives (pale red swellings), and itching
- Feeling of tightness in the chest and throat
- Swollen lips, face, ears, neck, and/or tongue
- Whistling or **WHEEZING** noises when breathing, changes in voice
- Nausea and/or vomiting

CHECK the scene and the child.

The child you are babysitting ate a nut. He or she is allergic to nuts. The child is having trouble breathing, and the lips and eyes are swelling.

CALL EMS/9-1-1 for help.

CARE

1. Help the child take any medication from the allergy kit (e.g., EpiPen®), or use his or her inhaler as necessary. Ask "yes" and "no" questions so the child can nod answers.

2. Open a window for fresh air.

3. Keep the child as comfortable as possible.

4. Continue to monitor the child's breathing.

Asthma

ASTHMA is a serious breathing problem often brought on by something a child is allergic to. Find out what you should do if a child you are caring for has an asthma attack. Ask parents if the child has an inhaler or machine (nebulizer), and find out when and how it should be used.

Signs of an asthma attack:

- Fast, shallow breathing and coughing
- Child says they can't breathe
- Child is confused, afraid, or nervous
- Child is dizzy, feels numb, has tingly fingers and toes
- A whistling, wheezing noise when the child breathes out

CHECK the scene and the child.

You know that the child you are babysitting has asthma. After a walk through the park he or she is wheezing a lot.

CALL EMS/9-1-1 for help.

CARE

1. Help the child use the inhaler as necessary.

2. Open a window for fresh air.

3. Keep the child as comfortable as possible.

4. If breathing does not improve, call EMS/9-1-1 for help if you have not already called.

5. Continue to monitor the child's breathing.

Seizures

Seizures may be caused by epilepsy or a high fever. Seizures can cause the child to lose control of his or her body and its movements.

CHECK the scene and the child.

CALL

Have someone else call EMS/9-1-1.

CARE

1. Move any furniture that is in the way that could hurt the child. Don't try and stop or control his or her movements.

2. Protect the head by putting a cushion or some folded clothing under it.

3. If there is saliva, blood, or vomit in the child's mouth, roll him or her into the recovery position.

4. Don't put anything between the child's teeth; an object could obstruct the AIRWAY.

5. After the seizure, if the child is unconscious, roll him or her into the recovery position. Call EMS/9-1-1 for help.

6. If the child is conscious, he or she may be tired and seem confused. Stay with the child and reassure him or her.

7. Call the parents or neighbour whose number you've been given.

Bee Stings

The child you are babysitting is playing in the back-yard and is stung by a bee.

CHECK the scene and the child.

You find a red, swollen spot (and stinger) where the bee stung the child.

CALL

Call EMS/9-1-1 if the child has a severe allergic reaction.

CARE

1. If you can see the stinger, scrape it away from the skin with your fingernail or a stiff card. Don't use tweezers because you may squeeze more poison into the child.

2. Wash the bite with soap and water and cover it to keep it clean.

3. Put a COLD PACK over the sting to reduce pain and swelling.

4. Watch the child for signs of an allergic reaction (difficulty breathing or a lot of swelling).

First Aid Kit

What's in a First Aid Kit?

All homes should have a first aid kit. Ask the parents where their first aid kit is, or bring your own so you can also take it on outings or to the park. Make sure the first aid kit is out of reach of children.

First aid kits should have the following things in them:

1. Emergency phone numbers

2. Small and large sterile gauze pads

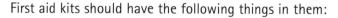

3. Adhesive tape

4. Bandages to make a sling

5. Adhesive bandages in assorted sizes

6. Scissors

7. Tweezers

8. Safety pins

9. Ice bag or chemical ice pack

10. Flashlight with extra batteries in a separate bag

11. Antiseptic wipes or soap

12. Pencil and paper

13. Emergency blanket

14. Barrier devices (e.g., disposable gloves and pocket mask or face shield)

15. Eye patches

16. Thermometer

17. Coins for pay phone. Remember, though, you don't need money to dial 9-1-1 at a pay phone.

18. Canadian Red Cross *First Aid & CPR Manual*

19. Comfort toy (e.g., small teddy bear)

Notes:

_____

_____

_____

_____

_____

Activity Page

Find the Word

Coins

Antiseptic wipes

Scissors

Paper

Tweezers

Pencil

Bandages

Blanket

Gloves

Thermometer

Flashlight

Tape

```
A F L A S H L I G H T A C E B
R N L Q O A E E V P S L O C A
A B T W E E Z E R S I Q M N N
O T H I V I Q D E C F F L J D
J K E O S L H A N R S V T Q A
E R R A E E B E C K M O V I G
S O M M T Q P A P E R P I J E
A C O F E P A T G I J K P R S
T V M X Y B D T I F G J L U K
V M E O C D E U S C K M N O P
P M T E E K V U J O W P L V Q
A C E E N G I K M I O I Q S U
O N R A K H G E C N A X P Y W
Q G L O V E S T U S Y W X E A
C B M O D E P S C I S S O R S
```

106

Special Considerations

Appropriate and Inappropriate Touching

Touch is important to the development and well-being of children. Appropriate touch is respectful, caring, kind, and safe. An appropriate touch can be an arm around the shoulder, holding hands, a gentle pat on the back, or a warm hug.

There are many situations in which you will have to touch the children you babysit. Babies will need to have their diapers changed, and younger children may need help going to the bathroom or getting dressed. Respect their feelings and give them only the help they need. If they are old enough to understand, always tell them what you need to do and ask their permission.

Remember, a child's body belongs to the child. Their bodies, like their feelings, need care, gentleness, and respect. If a child says "No!" to your touch, you must respect this unless his or her life is at risk. There are many examples of appropriate and inappropriate touch:

APPROPRIATE TOUCH

Changing diapers

Bathing children if unable to do it themselves

Cleaning children's genital and anal areas if unable to do it themselves

Holding a baby while bottle-feeding

Carrying a baby or young child

If the child agrees:

- An arm around the shoulder
- Holding hands
- A gentle pat on the back
- A warm hug

INAPPROPRIATE TOUCH

Touching children against their will

Touching children when you are angry, frustrated, or annoyed

Tickling children against their will

Shaking babies and children

Hitting or spanking children

Touching children's private areas (genital and anal areas) for purposes other than cleanliness

Kissing on the lips

Having children touch your private areas (breasts, genital and anal areas)

Child Abuse and Neglect

- CHILD ABUSE is when someone hurts a child physically, emotionally, or sexually.
- Child neglect is when someone does not take care of a child properly.

Possible signs of a physically abused child:

- Bruises and welts on the back, bottom, legs, upper arms, head, or face
- Old and new scars
- Burn marks
- Bite marks
- Missing hair

Physically abused children may be afraid of physical contact. They may try to hide their bruises and scars or make many excuses for them. Some children may be very aggressive and angry; others may be shy and fearful.

Too often, babies and children are hurt because they have been shaken. This is very dangerous, as a shaken baby or child may be seriously hurt or die. NEVER SHAKE A BABY OR CHILD!!

Possible signs of a neglected child:

- Constant hunger
- Dirtiness beyond usually playing
- Deep tiredness
- Inappropriate clothing
- Lack of medical attention

Physically neglected children may look unwell with no energy. Some are "clingy," while others may be very demanding.

Possible signs of an emotionally abused child:

- Depression
- No confidence
- Very aggressive or very passive
- Many temper tantrums
- Lots of crying and sulking

Possible signs of a sexually abuse child:

- Physical injuries in genital or anal area
- Too much knowledge about sex
- Talks a lot about sex
- Fearful of physical contact
- Fearful to undress
- Anger

What Do You Do?

1. Don't question the child yourself.

2. Tell an adult you trust about what you are seeing, hearing, or thinking.

3. Decide together if you need to contact child protection or police.

Remember it is very important that you talk to an adult.

Conclusion

Questions:

- What did you learn about yourself during this course?

- What will you take with you to be a great babysitter?

_____

_____

_____

_____

_____

_____

_____

_____

_____

_____

_____

_____

_____

_____

_____

Glossary

AIRWAY: The pathway through which air moves from the mouth and nose to the lungs.

ALLERGY: A negative reaction of the body to certain insect stings, foods, or medications.

ASTHMA: A condition that narrows the air passages and causes trouble breathing.

BABIES: Children younger than 12 months old.

CHECK, CALL, CARE: Three action steps you take in an emergency.

CHILD ABUSE: The physical, psychological, or sexual assault on a child, resulting in injury or emotional trauma.

CHOKING: A life-threatening emergency where the airway is partially or completely blocked. If the airway is completely blocked, an infant or child cannot cough, speak, cry, or breathe.

COLD PACK: A waterproof package containing ice or other frozen solids used in first aid to prevent or reduce swelling.

CONSCIOUS: When a person is awake or has not fainted.

CUT: A break in the skin's surface.

DEVELOPMENTAL STAGES: The stages a person goes through from birth to old age; each stage involves physical, mental, emotional, and social changes.

DISPATCHER: Emergency phone operator who can send medical, police, or fire personnel to assist with an emergency.

DISPOSABLE GLOVES: Thin, waterproof gloves worn to keep germs off the hands when contacting any body fluid, such as blood or vomit.

DIVERSITY: The differences found among people and their lifestyles.

DROWNING: Death by suffocating in water.

EMERGENCY: A problem situation where action is needed right away because someone is injured or ill.

ENVIRONMENT: Surrounding or condition.

FIRST AID: Care given to someone who is hurt or sick until more advanced care can be obtained. When provided in the first few minutes of an emergency, it can save a life.

FORMULA: A milk-based or soybean-based liquid mixture given to infants using a bottle.

HYGIENE: Activities like brushing your teeth or washing your hair and hands that help keep your body clean and healthy.

LEADERSHIP: Acting responsibly and taking charge of a situation.

NAUSEA: The feeling that can occur before vomiting. Feeling sick to the stomach.

POISONING: Eating, drinking, breathing, or injecting a solid, liquid, or gas that can injure or even kill you when taken into the body or put on the surface of the skin.

PRESCHOOLERS: Children three to five years old.

PROFESSIONAL: Being responsible, mature, reliable, and skillful.

RECOVERY POSITION: Lying on one side with the face angled toward the ground to protect and maintain an open airway in case of vomiting.

RÉSUMÉ: A list of one's experience, skills, and abilities for performing a job.

ROLE MODEL: Someone who acts in a responsible way for others to imitate.

SCHOOL-AGED CHILDREN: Children five years and older.

SCRAPE: A wound where the skin has been rubbed away.

SEIZURES: Trembling, shaking, or falling to the ground because of disturbed electrical output in the brain. This can be caused by an ongoing health problem, such as epilepsy, poisoning, a high fever, or a head injury.

SEVERE BLEEDING: Bleeding that squirts from the wound or cannot be stopped easily.

STERILE: Free from germs.

SUPERVISING: Staying with the child, with your eyes on the child as much as possible.

TODDLERS: Children one to three years old.

TOILETING: Urinating or having a bowel movement into a toilet. A child usually is toilet trained between two to five years of age.

UNCONSCIOUS: When a person is not awake or has fainted. The person is not aware of his or her surroundings.

VOMIT: To throw up what is in the stomach through the mouth.

WHEEZING: A hoarse, whistling sound during breathing that usually signals a breathing problem.

WOUND: An injury to the body.

Resources

As you gain experience as a professional babysitter, you should always strive to become a better babysitter. One way of becoming a better babysitter is to get new and the most up-to-date information. Below are some internet resources you can check out on child safety tips and the latest in babysitting.

- Canadian Red Cross www.redcross.ca

- American Red Cross www.redcross.org

- Health Canada www.hc-sc.gc.ca

- Safe Kids Canada www.safekidscanada.ca

- Canadian Health Network
  www.canadian-health-network.ca

- Fire Prevention Canada www.fiprecan.ca

First Aid and CPR Training

This course does not provide you with certification in First Aid and CPR. It does provide you with some knowledge and skill practice in these areas. It is always a good idea to get more training. If you want certification, it is recommended that you enroll in a Canadian Red Cross First Aid & CPR course.

Call your local Red Cross or 1-877-356-3226 for more information on available courses.

Notes:

Notes:

Notes:

Notes:

Notes: